Social Darwinism

Current Titles

Concepts in the Social Sciences

Social Darwinism

Linking Evolutionary Thought to Social Theory

Peter Dickens

Open University Press
Buckingham · Philadelphia

Open University Press
Celtic Court
22 Ballmoor
Buckingham
MK18 1XW

email: enquiries@openup.co.uk
world wide web: http://www.openup.co.uk

and
325 Chestnut Street
Philadelphia, PA 19106, USA

First Published 2000

A catalogue record of this book is available from the British Library

ISBN 0 335 20218 7 (pb)   0 335 20219 5 (hb)

Library of Congress Cataloging-in-Publication Data
Dickens, Peter, 1940–
      Social Darwinism : linking evolutionary thought to social theory /
Peter Dickens.
          p.   cm. — (Concepts in the social sciences)
      Includes bibliographical references and index.
      ISBN 0-335-20219-5 (hb)   —   ISBN 0-335-20218-7 (pbk.)
      1. Social Darwinism   I. Title.   II. Series.
   HM631.D53   2000
   301—dc21   99-056450

Typeset by Type Study, Scarborough
Printed in Great Britain by St Edmundsbury Press, Bury St Edmunds,
Suffolk

For Paul and Chris

Contents

Acknowledgements

An interdisciplinary project of this kind means acknowledgements are due in a number of directions. Andrew Chitty, Lee Freese, Andrew Whiten and Richard Wilkinson gave important assistance with particular parts of the book. Ted Benton and Bill Catton read the whole manuscript and made a number of very helpful suggestions. Many thanks also to David Barker, Alan Buckingham, Jenneth Parker and Pete Saunders.

Introduction: Unpacking 'Social Darwinism'

The notion of 'social Darwinism' refers to a complex range of ideas. It is important to be clear about these. Which are likely to be useful in understanding the relations between sociological and evolutionary ideas and which are not?

First, let us consider Darwinian biology. As is well known, Darwin asserted that biological laws affect all living beings, human beings included. Population growth in the context of limited resources leads to a struggle for survival, again amongst all living organisms. Certain physical and mental characteristics confer advantages and disadvantages to individuals in the struggle for survival. The selection of these traits and their inheritance over time will in due course lead to the emergence of new species and the elimination of others.

The application of these ideas to human societies, however, has taken a number of forms – and it is at this point that the difficulties begin. Perhaps the least contentious extension to human beings is the suggestion that we are not only animals but cultural animals; that our social and political institutions, our ethics and religion, are linked to our evolutionary development. So human nature may be special in all sorts of ways but it can, this position asserts, still be linked back to evolutionary thought and its extension to human beings. Precisely how this link is to be made is still open to debate. There are some extremely difficult analytical and political questions about how social relations and social systems either impede or encourage the development of human capacities. This problematic terrain is entered into later.

So far, perhaps, so good. But 'social Darwinism' has been taken much further than this. For example, as we will shortly see, it has been suggested (and in some quarters is still being suggested) that human social organization is itself a kind of human organism. Like other natural organisms, it can be seen as undergoing developmental change. It seems to become, for example, increasingly differentiated into distinct yet connected parts. At this stage, one in which there appears to be a kind of superorganic force applying to society as well as to nature, the whole idea of social Darwinism starts running into very severe trouble. In the end we are dealing with rather mystical analogies which may be offering little genuine understanding.

Social Darwinism runs into the greatest difficulties, however, when policy prescriptions are drawn from over-simple ideas regarding people's biologically-based behaviours. It is on this point that social Darwinism has justifiably developed its bad reputation. In particular, it has been closely linked to eugenics, with eugenic planning. Like town planning (but doing far more harm), it was a concept used to justify making a new and ordered society. As an accelerated form of natural selection, eugenics was intended to culminate with a better race. And who makes such an ordered society? It was to be a social elite, the kind of people whose stock was most worth reproducing into future generations. Such a conclusion has been reached by political right and left alike. (Box 1). It finds echoes today with the horrendous 'ethnic cleansing' in which a Serbian elite has been expelling and killing thousands of Croats and Muslims.

Some commentators now see the possibility of new and more subtle kinds of eugenics in Western societies whereby genetic discoveries will be used towards the construction of supposedly ideal people. Wealthy middle-class parents may, for example, attempt to create 'designer children'. Insurance companies may refuse to offer cover to people with genetic propensities to certain kinds of illness. People with a genetic predisposition to certain illnesses may not get jobs. All these interventions not only raise a host of ethical issues, but there is every chance that they will not work as intended. People's illnesses, for example, are as much a product of their environment as they are of particular genes. Nevertheless, this can

---

Box 1 Social Darwinism as persecution

We must be able to pick out the genetically inferior stocks with more certainty, and we must set in motion counter-forces making for faster reproduction of superior stocks. . . . Neither of these is possible without an alteration of the social system.

(Julian Huxley, cited in Bland and Doan 1998: 198)

Providence has endowed living creatures with a limitless fecundity; but she has not put in their reach, without the need for effort on their part, all the food they need. All that is very right and proper, for it is the struggle for existence that produces the selection of the fittest.

(Adolf Hitler, cited in Hawkins 1997: 274)

Those who thought the pseudo-science of eugenics had been finally discredited by its association with Hitler have been astonished and dismayed to learn that Sweden, that paradise of social democracy, sterilised thousands of misfits and social deviants of both sexes in order to produce a better breed of Swede and a socially responsible citizenry.

(*The Scotsman*, 3 September 1997)

---

be seen as a future form of eugenics: the manipulation of biology to create a perfect human race.

But why further discuss such a discredited and still dangerous concept? Is there any more to a book on social Darwinism beyond exploring how Darwin's ideas have been reconstructed, used and misused by socially dominant groups of people to control others such as women and 'other' races? Is there any more to reasserting, for example, that there is no biological reality to the concept of race and that it remains, in Ashley Montagu's (1997) well-known words, 'man's most dangerous myth'?

But there is some value in a notion of social Darwinism if we return to the meanings with which this introduction started. In particular, we need to explore the implications of Darwin's original tenets (and of those of some of his intellectual successors) regarding human beings and their societies. In other words, the need now is to penetrate behind the least satisfactory and at times horrific applications of Darwinian thought and return to somewhere near the point where Darwin himself started. This is of course a massive task, but the effort is well worth making.

Chapter 1 explores some of the origins of social Darwinism. It contrasts Darwin's own 'social Darwinism' with that adopted by social scientists themselves. The picture is one in which the social scientists' form of social Darwinism was indeed often used as a tool against relatively powerless people and a means of justifying racism and sexism. It also shows that the themes of 'progress', 'direction' and 'teleology' were often implicit in early social thought which used evolutionary ideas as its inspiration. Such applications are at the very least suspect and had little to do with evolution as understood by natural scientists. On the other hand, some early writers influenced by Darwinian thought (Marx and Engels in particular) started to make important connections between society and nature, connections which remain particularly important to us today. Chapter 2 argues, however, that many of the less helpful themes derived from evolutionary thought persist in modern social theory. Furthermore, they are still often based on flawed analogies between evolution in nature on the one hand and that of human society on the other. Many of these analogies are highly questionable. One of the chief problems of social Darwinism as it has developed since Darwin's day has been the rising dualism between society on the one hand and nature on the other. The two rarely meet except, again, in the form of analogies. Such analogizing is in the end unhelpful. Paradoxically, however, it is a key feature of those biologists who now claim to be 'neo-Darwinians'. Chapter 3 pursues this matter in relation to current social analysis of the underclass and its supposed genetically inherited characteristics. This work raises the very important question of what Marx called human 'species-being', people's natural limits, propensities and potentials. But it is at the same time problematic, mainly because it reproduces the old dualism between society and nature: it fails to relate social processes and relations on the one hand to people's biologically inherited capacities on the other. Chapter 4 discusses this matter and begins to suggest how work might be carried out to create a more satisfactory fusion of evolutionary and social thought – one which starts to overcome the dualism between society and nature and one which could return to the kind of unified position outlined by Darwin himself. Humans, it is suggested, are culture-making animals. They are what Wills (1993) calls 'knowledge sponges', designed to develop an understanding of one another and of nature as they interact with the social and natural world. They are able to undertake a process of self-evolution, enabling them to consciously develop new concepts, new understandings, which facilitate new forms of interaction. They are a natural sort, and a culture-making natural sort. This leads to Chapter 5 which discusses recent research on 'human nature'. Have human individuals evolved as ruthlessly competitive or collectively-oriented? Or are they, as this chapter suggests, neither of these? This chapter concludes by arguing that the essence of human nature is the power of abstraction, and the capacity to link general ideas to practical activity. This leads to Chapter 6, which pulls together a number of the book's themes. It sketches a way in which social and evolutionary thought can start to be combined. Such a combination can be made by fusing historical materialism with forms of biology which focus on organisms rather than genes. These latter disciplines are emerging as especially helpful as regards understanding what human 'species-being' actually is and how the development of people during their lifetimes links to longer-term evolutionary processes. Again, the power for abstraction emerges as central to the development of people during their lifetimes. But this potential can be, and has been, realized or changed by the environmental or social context within which they are developing. This brings us to capitalism. The rise of the capitalist mode of production has clearly brought great benefits, particularly in terms of material well-being for large numbers of people. But it is becoming increasingly clear that the realization of human potential (including the potential for living a long and healthy life) is considerably influenced by social relations and processes. Impacts on the developing child are especially important. Control over human capacities may be leading to illness amongst many people on the receiving end of this process.

Merging evolutionary thought with social theory is therefore concerned both with people's genetically inherited capacities and with the many and varied attempts of the powerful to control these powers. At the same time it is concerned with struggles 'from below' to realize these same capacities. But how is human biology itself evolving as a result of these processes? Very little is known about this connection but recent developments in the life sciences suggest that the exercise of social power could even be having important long-term effects on human biology and perhaps even on human evolution itself. The cult science fiction movie *Bladerunner* looked ahead to a twenty-first-century capitalism in which a special group of (mutinous) slaves has been genetically manufactured. Perhaps such a future is already in place, though not as a result of interventions by malevolent biotechnologists. The new kind of 'social Darwinism' sketched out here suggests an exciting research programme spanning the social and political sciences. Like *Bladerunner*, it is also charged with major political implications.

1
Social Darwinism: Problems of Direction, Purpose and Progress

The first edition of Darwin's *Origin of Species by Means of Natural Selection* was published in 1859. Its influence was profound not only for the natural sciences but also for the study of human beings and their social relationships. This chapter, after a brief account of Darwin's theory and the social context in which it was developed, outlines the various ways in which the theory was extended by Darwin and by many of the classical social theorists to the study of human society. As we will see, some of these ways now seem much more helpful than others.

Relationships between *Origin of Species* on the one hand and the natural and social sciences on the other were more complex than is often supposed. Exploring 'social Darwinism' and the application of Darwin's evolutionary ideas to the human social world is a complex matter, not least because a well-developed form of what might be called 'social Darwinism' actually preceded the publication of Darwin's book (Hawkins 1997). Similarly, early forms of evolutionary thought were well established and debated some time before Darwin's book was published. The ideas of Lamarck (incorporating the thesis that characteristics acquired by an organism could be inherited by its progeny) and of Geoffroy (who argued that there was a basic underlying morphology to all animals) were, for example, widely discussed during the early nineteenth century. In fact these French scientists were made into ideological rallying points for socialists, atheists and a new generation of scientists in London who were resisting the power of scientific and religious authority (Desmond 1989). All this well before *The Origin of Species*. And even when Darwin directly influenced social theory, only parts of his thinking were taken up and developed. It is also important to note that *The Origin* itself contained certain assumptions which were a product of Darwin's own society.

Most living creatures, Darwin's book argued, produce many more offspring than is needed to simply reproduce their numbers. Unless encountering resistance from limiting factors within its environment a population would tend to increase in geometric ratio:

> There is no exception to the rule that every organic being naturally increases at so high a rate, that if not destroyed, the earth would soon be covered by the progeny of a single pair. Even slow-breeding man has doubled in twenty-five years, and at this rate, in a few thousand years, there would literally not be standing room for his progeny.
>
> (Darwin 1968: 117)

Yet despite this, the number of any one species remains, according to Darwin, much the same from one generation to another. It therefore followed that a struggle for survival had to take place. This struggle included not only competition for the young to achieve maturity but also success in leaving progeny. And it also included, as Darwin (1968: 116) was careful to point out, not only outright competition but also 'dependence of one being on another'.

Change in species was central to Darwin's theory. No two individuals are alike, all showing variation in some way or other. And these variations, which were blind, randomly produced and therefore haphazard, confer both advantages and disadvantages in the struggle for survival. Those individuals with given advantages will become fully developed and will reproduce future generations. Those without these advantages will fail in these respects. The overall picture is one of a common set of parents giving rise to immense variation over vastly long periods of evolutionary time:

> The innumerable species, genera, and families of organic beings, with which this world is peopled, have all descended, each within its own class or group, from common parents, and have all been modified in the course of descent.
>
> (Darwin 1968: 434)

The minute variations in the organization of an organism were largely induced, according to *The Origin*, by reproduction. But Darwin also envisaged other processes combining with this central mechanism. These include, he argued, sexual selection. Darwin believed that some of the physical forms and behavioural dispositions of animals could be best explained by such processes such as courtship displays and physical features intended to attract the opposite sex. Physical variation was also seen by Darwin as to some small degree created by changing environmental conditions and by the use and disuse of organs. These particular explanations formed only a very small part of *The Origin*, but it is important to record them here since they point to Darwin's refusal to understand evolution with reference to just one factor and they were later to become a much more important part of Darwin's theorizing. As regards the importance of the use and disuse or organs, note, for example, the following in the conclusion to *The Origin*:

> Disuse, aided sometimes by natural selection, will often tend to reduce an organ, when it has become useless by changed habits or under changed conditions of life; and we can clearly understand on this view the meaning of rudimentary organs.
>
> (Darwin 1968: 451)

Darwin's book is a scientific treatise. This needs to be remembered in the context of the trend in our own era to analyse science as only a social construct and incapable of referring to a real external world. Darwin claimed to have uncovered real causal mechanisms in the natural (and, by extension, human) worlds. Darwin's work was a product of its times (Gruber 1974; Hawkins 1997; Trigger 1998). He was directly inspired by, for example, Malthus's *Essay on Population*, written in 1798. The Malthusian theory, which was developed for understanding human societies, purported to show that while population grows geometrically, food supplies grow arithmetically unless checked by famine, war, disease or some other such constraint. Such a theory was informed, however, by a particular and dominant set of values, one which attributes relatively little significance to social relations between members of the population. Resource shortages may not be only a product of social relations, but it is misleading to discuss resource limits separately from questions of social and political power (for a discussion, see Benton 1991). Darwin joined many of his Victorian contemporaries in accepting Malthus's ideas as if they were unencumbered by social and political questions.

Note the alternative scenario developed by Alfred Russell Wallace. Wallace is best known as the independent discoverer of the theory of evolution and the naturalist whose sketch of the theory of natural selection hastened Darwin into publishing *The Origin of Species*. Debates have ensued as to whether Wallace's originality has been consistently underestimated. Perhaps because he was socially less well connected and because he spent much of his time doing research in Amazonia and Malaya, his innovatory role has never been properly recognized. Perhaps more important than these debates over originality, however, are his political priorities and in particular his attitude to Malthus, an author with whom he was familiar. Wallace's views were particularly influenced by an earlier encounter with Owenite socialism, which led him to place much greater emphasis on social relations and processes associated with population growth and shortage of food and resources. In particular, he argued that the division of labour and power relations between the sexes and within the population as a whole was the key factor affecting population numbers and material well-being. He recognized, however, that while the division of labour brought new social conflicts, it also brought about real material advantages. The laborious work he observed in the Amazon region was, for example,

> principally the result of everybody doing everything for himself, slowly and with much unnecessary labour, instead of occupying himself with one kind of industry and exchanging its produce for the articles he requires . . . the consequence is that his work produces but sixpence a week and he is therefore all his life earning a scanty supply of clothing in a country where food may be had almost for nothing.
>
>   (Wallace 1869, cited in Jones 1980)

But despite the differences between Wallace and Darwin (to which we will shortly return) it is important to note here that both were pointing to real causal processes and that the theory of natural selection has largely stood the test of time. It is a good theory, despite the fact that it was 'socially constructed'.

Darwin and Wallace are perhaps best known for confronting Victorian Christianity and the idea of God's creation of the world. To many people, including the clergy and those scientists who believed that God created the world and all its forms, *The Origin of Species* was clearly blasphemous. The idea of the struggle for survival and the design of species being accounted for by small, chance variations meant there was no longer space for divine intervention. Furthermore, the suggestion that humans shared common ancestors (an implication which was clear from *The Origin*, though not fully sketched out until *The Descent of Man*) was directly indicated by Darwin's book. The reaction of the Church to Darwin is perhaps best summed up with the words of one clergyman: 'He is the most dangerous man in Europe' (cited in Overy 1997: 56).

Given such apparent opposition, it comes as little surprise to learn that Darwin decided to take the waters in Ilkley, far away from London, on the day his book was published. Since 1838, when he had first developed his theory, he had anticipated adverse reaction and, as is widely known, that is one of the reasons why he delayed publishing so long. On the other hand, given the hostile response from the religious establishment, it perhaps comes as some surprise that all 1250 copies of the first edition of *The Origin* were sold out on the first day of its publication. Why should this be?

The book made immediate contact with a wide public not just because, as is often said, it was deliberately written with a non-specialist readership in mind. The opening chapter on the role of animal and plant breeders in effecting domesticated forms of selection was certainly a brilliant way of leading into the theory of natural selection. But the book's popularity was also due to the fact that it was a theory which had been 'socially constructed'. It also chimed in well with many of the concerns and priorities of the time. In particular, intellectuals writing books on evolution were again reflecting the values of industrialists and commercialists of Victorian Britain. Even though it should be treated as, above all else, a book of science, there remain in the book distinct traces of its social origins.

These centre on three distinct themes: *progress*, *teleology* and *direction*. Note that while they are distinct, these concepts also overlap in complex ways and are subject to change. A teleological view of the world, for example, explains outcomes with reference to underlying purposes. A structure or development of nature can, for example, be seen as evidence of the Creator's wisdom and benevolence. Up to the eighteenth and early nineteenth century, 'evolution' implied teleology or the unfolding of a pre-existing plan (Williams 1976a, 1976b). Teleology in this sense overlaps with 'progress'. But 'progress' entails a normative judgement, unless it refers (as it did before the rise of capitalism) to just a sequence of events, as in the 'progress' of a disease. Evolution can be held to have a direction (towards, for example, increasing differentiation), though whether this is 'progress' depends again on a normative judgement.

Darwin's theory did not explicitly depend on any of these themes. Indeed, his work was largely responsible for posing major critical questions regarding such assumptions – especially, of course, assumptions regarding teleology. Nevertheless, *The Origins* is somewhat ambivalent about these matters, even implicitly accepting them in places. This led to the book not only creating a high degree of controversy but also attracting a considerable degree of popular and scientific acceptance. On occasions in his book Darwin maintained, for example, that despite the struggle for existence, the outcome over the long term does result in some kind of progress:

> The inhabitants of each successive period in the world's history have beaten their predecessors in the race for life, and are, in so far, higher in the scale of nature; and this may account for that vague yet ill-defined sentiment, felt by many paleontologists, that organisation on the whole has progressed.
>
> (Ruse 1996: 152)

In *The Origin* we find the last chapter, 'The Struggle for Existence', combining both the notion of some direction to evolution over time as well as progress in the sense that some good is being achieved:

> When we reflect on this struggle we may console ourselves with the full belief, that the war of nature is not incessant, that no fear is felt, that death is generally prompt, and that the vigorous, the healthy, and the happy survive and multiply.
>
> (Darwin 1968: 129)

The issue of direction links closely to direction towards a particular or predetermined end. This again was not a central part of Darwin's theory. Indeed, Darwin can again be seen as one of the prime movers in challenging such thinking. Despite this, Darwin was addressing a puzzle which concerned many in his era, most obviously middle-class scientists and clerics (Ruse 1996). A sound scientific theory in the mid-nineteenth century had to explain why an organism was seemingly so well adapted to be precisely what it is. Natural selection provided a new and rational answer to an old question. Evolution was, in an apparently teleological way, 'directing' the organization and functioning of organisms.

As a scientist, therefore, Darwin can be seen as challenging dominant ways of thought in the nineteenth century. But, as we have seen, his theory was also a product of its time. Much the same can be said as regards the theory's relationships with Christianity. Darwin can be seen as delivering a fatal blow to Christian accounts of human origins. But many of the themes outlined above can be given a different interpretation. Far from abandoning Creationism, they can be seen as a new, scientific version of Creationism. The notion of the multiplicity of 'species, genera and families of organic beings' all having 'common parents' has, it need hardly be said, distinct biblical overtones. The notion of a plant or an animal realizing or unfolding its inborn potential can be similarly seen as containing a strong teleological element, even if not explicitly Christian. Progress despite harshness, a direction to evolution, and evolution as having some pre-given end of its own can all therefore be easily seen as secular versions of creationism, challenging religious ideas and yet subtly reproducing them (Bowler 1983). And the notion of a moral purpose to evolution (one which was only briefly alluded to by Darwin but which was developed much further by social Darwinists) made evolution into what Gellner (1988: 144) has called a God-surrogate.

Again, Darwinism can be seen as what is now called by many sociologists a 'social construction', the implicit suggestion being that his ideas are little more than a product of their time. It was a social construction, but that is not *all* that it was. It was above all a scientific theory, one describing real causal processes.

We are now almost at a stage to explore the emergence of an explicitly social Darwinism (or a Darwinism for human society) in more detail. This can be done in three ways: by examining how Darwin himself applied his theory to the human world; by looking at those forms of 'Social Darwinism' which preceded Darwin; and finally, by looking at the impact of Darwinism on later social and political thought.

Darwin's social Darwinism

Light will be thrown on the origin of man and his history.

(Darwin 1968: 458)

Darwin suggested, in this frequently repeated quotation at the end of *The Origin of Species*, that his theory of natural selection may have something to say about human beings and human societies. In addition, it is clear from his notebooks dating from the 1830s that an understanding of humanity had long been one of his chief concerns (Darwin 1987a, 1987b, 1987c). Wallace asked him before the publication of *The Origin* whether he had any plans to discuss human beings in his forthcoming book. It is clear from his response that Darwin anticipated too much trouble from entering into such a discussion. It would only deflect attention away from his main intention, that of developing his scientific theory.

> You ask whether I shall discuss 'man'. I think I shall avoid the whole subject, as so surrounded with prejudices; though I fully admit it is the highest and most interesting problem for the naturalist.
>
> (cited in Hawkins 1997: 20)

It was not, therefore, until the publication of *The Descent of Man* in 1871 that the world at large began to hear of Darwin's own 'social Darwinism'. The central and difficult project for Darwin, and indeed for anyone attempting an evolutionary understanding of human beings, is how to explain what appear to be the very distinctive and highly developed capacities of humans. How, in particular, should human powers of abstraction, language, sociality, morality and perhaps even their recurrent religiosity or spirituality be explained? If these qualities are not God-given, where did they come from? Wallace himself believed some supernatural guiding force must have been at work.

A similar set of questions surrounded the key problem of race during the time Darwin was writing (Box 2). If white, Western 'man' was not to be envisaged as a species distinct from black people how were the differences in the behaviours and mental development of different races to be explained? In the 1860s there was intense debate within Britain between the monogenists and polygenists (Jones 1980). The first group argued that there was a common ancestor for all human races, that humanity is all of a piece. The second argument was that different races are indeed separate species. The implication of the first argument was that certain human beings or races had simply not developed to become full humans in the European and Victorian sense. The implication of the second position was that many then contemporary races should be seen as still extant versions of earlier, inherently less developed, species. Such arguments, which are discussed in more detail in Box 2, may seem extremely suspect to us now, but Darwin could not help but be caught up by them and be influenced by them.

Box 2   Social Darwinism and race

Race was at the heart of attempts during the nineteenth century to construct a specifically social Darwinism. Evolutionism became caught up with a general concern about social change, imperialism and colonialism, about the tensions arising from rapid industrial change and about the long-term fate of nations (Stepan 1982; Barkan 1992; Malik 1996).

John Lubbock, who grew up as Darwin's neighbour, is often seen as the first social Darwinist (Trigger 1998). He is also famous (even infamous) for developing one of the first theories of race based on Darwin's ideas. He saw the cultural and biological development of races as having occurred in parallel, and as a result of natural selection. 'The whole history of man shows how', he wrote, 'the stronger and progressive, increase in numbers and drive out the weaker and lower races' (Lubbock 1875: 3) Modern Europeans, he argued, had developed to the point of dominance as a result of natural selection. They had struggled for their existence and had therefore developed as superior to 'savages'. Primitive peoples had remained superstitious, irrational and unable to handle abstract concepts. Their behaviour and attitudes were much the same as children in European societies. 'The mind of the savage, like that of a child, is easily fatigued, and he will then give random answers, to spare himself the trouble of thought' (Lubbock 1875: 9). These characteristics had led, Lubbock argued, to the inevitable destruction of non-European races.

Note in the above quotation the idea that the development of individuals during their lifetime echoes the whole of the evolutionary history of their species. This is known as 'recapitulation theory', a concept which was widely accepted in the nineteenth century.

Lubbock's theory, however, was only one way in which social Darwinism was applied to race. Herbert Spencer, for example, argued (in line with some religious leaders) that primitive peoples have probably degenerated from a more advanced state. Unlike Lubbock, he felt they cannot be seen as illustrations of earlier stages through which European people have passed. Meanwhile,

---

Box 2   *continued*

the evolutionary anthropologist Edward Tylor believed (at least in his earliest writings) in the uniformity of human nature, with early humans being primitive philosophers.

By the 1940s, however, 'scientific racism' became widely seen as a pseudo-science. Key thinkers, such as the biologist Julian Huxley, changed their minds over the category 'race', exposing it as little more than an attempt to give a scientific credibility to popular prejudice. 'The term "race"', he wrote in 1931, 'is often used as if "races" were definite biological entities, sharply marked off from each other. This is simply not true' (cited in Malik 1996: 125).

How, then, did Darwin attempt to develop his evolutionary perspective to include human beings and their society? His opening argument was that what appeared to be humans' distinctive capacities and potentials could be observed, albeit in less developed forms, in other species. Clearly, the differences between humans and other animals are immense but this does not rule out the possibility that we have highly advanced versions of what other animals have. According to Darwin, therefore, humans are definitely a natural sort and many of our predispositions are recognizable in other creatures. Of humans' mental capacities, for example, Darwin (1901: 193) writes:

> The difference in mind between man and the higher animals, great as it is, certainly is one of degree and not of kind. . . . The senses and intuitions, the various emotions and faculties, such as love, memory, attention, curiosity, imitation, reason, etc., of which man boasts, may be found in an incipient, or even sometimes in a well-developed condition, in the lower animals.

But simply asserting humans' continuity with other animals does not explain how humans (and other animals) came to have the capacities they have. The answer for Darwin lies, as might be expected, in their evolutionary history. Their distinctive capacities conferred particular advantages in the struggle for survival under pressure of population growth and limited resources. The capacity to step back from immediate activity, to reason, to communicate complex ideas, to support members of their own tribe can all be explained as an inheritance developed in the process of natural selection. So too can altruism. This too could be slowly bred into individuals as a means of protecting the tribe in the competition for resources, including the competition against other tribes. Therefore those who had these capacities would tend to be selected and those without them would not. As regards sociality, for example:

> [s]uch qualities, the paramount importance of which to the lower animals is disputed by no one, were no doubt acquired by the progenitors of man in a similar manner, namely, through natural selection, aided by inherited habit.

> (Darwin 1901: 199)

Note, however, Darwin's mention here of 'inherited habit'. In *The Origin*, as we have seen, Darwin attributed little significance to Lamarckism, the notion that changes in heredity could occur through the effort of an organism adapting to its environment and then passing on some of its self-created capacities to the next generation. With *The Descent of Man*, however, Darwin started to place a greater emphasis on the possibility of the inheritance of acquired characteristics. It is a view which finds little support in evolutionary science, though the suggestion is now once again receiving serious attention from a few natural scientists. However, Lamarckism was an important feature of much evolutionary thought in the mid-nineteenth century.

Darwin's theory underwent further development when it came to the question of race in *The Descent*. In line with his general theory, he believed that all extant human beings came of the same origins. Furthermore, he accepted (on the basis of research by Lubbock, Morgan, Tylor and others) that 'all civilised nations were once barbarous' but that 'some savages have recently improved a little in some of their simpler arts' (Darwin 1901: 221). (See also Trigger 1998.) Such statements not only tacitly imply judgements regarding progress and directionality to human development, they can also be read as implying that 'civilization' in the form of the white imperializing nations represented some kind of end-point to which the whole of evolution was tending. And, to today's eyes, there is more than a hint of racism in Darwin's work. He accepted, for example, the arguments and measurements of contemporary phrenologists suggesting that brain size is an indication of intelligence (Bowler 1990). Nevertheless, a closer reading of *The Descent* suggests we should again try to locate him in the context of contemporary debates. His main concern was to confront theories which were inspired by religion and which had, he believed, little empirical backing.

> The arguments recently advanced by the Duke of Argyll and formerly by Archbishop Whately, in favour of the belief that man came into the world as a civilised being, and that all savages have since undergone degradation, seem to me weak in comparison with those advanced on the other side.
>
> (Darwin 1901: 221)

One of the main features of *The Descent*, and one which distinguished it from *The Origin*, was an extra emphasis on sexual selection. This took more than one form in Darwin's analysis. The suggestion was that in much the same way as males of other species struggle for females, human males competed to be the best warrior, the best hunter, in order to attract the greatest number of wives. In this way, and again including some assumptions about Lamarckian inheritance, Darwin saw intelligence and muscular power developed particularly amongst males. But sexual selection was also used by Darwin to account for the physical differences of races. In *The Descent* Darwin declares himself 'baffled' in accounting for 'the differences between the races of man'. Neither natural selection nor the continued exercise of certain body-parts could alone account for the different colours or physical characteristics of human beings throughout the world. He suggests, however, that 'there remains one important agency, namely Sexual Selection, which appears to have acted powerfully on man, as on many other animals' (Darwin 1901: 307–8). In short, variation is not simply the product of natural selection but of different physical traits being selected in the process of human mating.

In these ways, then, Darwin built up his own type of social Darwinism. His emphasis on the commonality of all human beings and the spectrum of humans and other animals was to be taken up and further developed in *The Expression of the Emotions in Man and Animals* (Darwin 1998). It was an argument which in the end proved largely irresistible. Nevertheless, as we have also seen, his arguments and values (especially those implying some kind of progress, directionality and even an underlying purpose to evolution) were necessarily a product of his time. It is to these arguments, many of which had their origins before Darwin's day, to which we must now turn.

Theories of social evoltuion: analogies with nature or society as part of nature?

Herbert Spencer coined the term 'survival of the fittest' some ten years before Darwin's *Origin of Species*. Indeed, according to one Spencer enthusiast, Darwin should be nominated as a 'biological Spencerian' in preference to continuing to call Spencer a 'social Darwinist' (Turner 1985). But the fact also is that forms of evolutionary thought were well established in social theory well before even Spencer. But before coming to Spencer, we should briefly outline some forms of evolutionary thought which were an important feature of early social theory and of evolutionary theory contemporary with Spencer. The themes of progress, direction and teleology emerge here as even more important than they did in Darwin's work. But in engaging with theories of social evolution we encounter a major methodological issue. Should we envisage these theories using the natural world as mere analogies – suggesting, that is, that social change has parallels in the natural world? Or is the suggestion that human society is indeed part of nature, and that the same forces and processes involved in the natural world also affect human society? This key issue particularly comes to the fore with the work of Herbert Spencer, but we need to discuss earlier authors who also made analogies between human and natural society.

For Hegel (1770–1831) world history is a process of increasing understanding by people of the society in which they live (Hegel 1975). The first stages of such understanding were based simply on the senses – sight, smell and touch. Later, people started to understand themselves and the potentials they possessed which were capable of further realization. But this led to a conflict between what people were and what they could become. Social change, Hegel suggested, stems from people not only becoming conscious of society's prevailing ideas or 'spirit' but also acting to become part of that spirit. In so far as they achieved that integration, people become fully-fledged human beings. As they become part of history it becomes integral to them. They become an unalienated species, one in which they become recognized *as* human beings: 'the expression of the divine and absolute process of the spirit in its highest forms, of the progression whereby it discovers its true nature and becomes conscious of itself' (Hegel 1975: 65).

For Hegel, then, world history entailed a definite sequence and

progression. It also contains a strong sense of climax, of some ideal
to which world history has always been aiming. Something of the
same sense of progress and direction applies to early French sociology, and particularly to Comte (1798–1857). His evolutionary
theory consisted of the law of the three stages. As in Hegel, the
stages are defined in terms of dominant ideas helping human beings
to understand their circumstances. The first, 'theological' stage was
dominated by supernatural and religious ideas. In the second,
'metaphysical' stage, lasting between about 1300 and 1800, explanation of events was largely via abstract forces such as 'nature'.
Finally, from about 1800 onwards religious and metaphysical explanations are abandoned as scientific laws based on detailed empirical observation become the dominant way of seeing the world.
Comte envisaged the new science of sociology (one based on the
older physical and natural sciences) as actively contributing to this
stage. Again, there are clear notions in this picture of direction,
progress and even of an implied preordained outcome to intellectual evolution.

Like Hegel, Comte and other writers we will consider later,
Spencer was searching for general laws which underly social
change. In this sense he too was trying to emulate the physical and
natural sciences. But he was far more thoroughgoing in this respect
than any other social scientist before or after his time. This was
because he was not only trying to find laws affecting social change;
in much of his writing he argues that laws of the physical and
natural world were directly impinging on human affairs.

Spencer's vast corpus of work makes him quite difficult to sum-
marize. Indeed, one author has suggested that his work contained
at least four distinct theories of social evolution (Perrin 1976). This
makes his work something of a moving target, but it is nevertheless
possible to outline some of its main themes. First, Spencer's evolutionary thought was as much linked to physics as to biology. They
both stemmed from the principle of the conservation of energy or
what he called the 'persistence of force' (Hawkins 1997). Spencer
envisaged the whole universe as in a state of constant flux. Such
constant change derived from the 'instability of the homogeneous'.
Persistent force on homogeneous matter constantly leads, he
argued, to the development of more structured complexity, with
parts becoming more differentiated and at the same time more inte-
grated with one another. This principle applies to the whole of

nature, and indeed to human society itself. In the case of organic nature, for example, organisms are constantly struggling to survive, to build relationships between themselves and their environment. The organism undergoes change in order to adapt to the force to which it is submitted. And in its attempt to achieve a balance with its environment it becomes more differentiated and composed of connected parts. This 'direct equilibration' was accompanied by natural selection, the survival of the fittest.

In Spencer's version of 'social Darwinism' the weakest members of what he called a 'race' (this term referred not just to human races but, in a general sense, to a subspecies or variety) will die out and the strongest will survive and reproduce. Furthermore, they will tend to reproduce their characteristics into the next generation.

> The average vigour of any race would be diminished did the diseased and feeble habitually survive and propagate; and . . . the destruction of such, through failure to fulfil some of the conditions to life, leaves behind those who are able to fulfil the conditions to life, and thus keeps up the average fitness to the conditions of life.
> (Spencer 1898: 532–3, cited by Hawkins 1997)

The analysis extended into Spencer's views on the role of women. On the one hand, he realized that women's capacities (especially their mental capacities) go unrecognized and that men were concerned more for women's appearance than for their mental abilities. At the same time, he argued that the monogamous family composed of the housewife, working man and children was the most efficient and progressive form of human organization (Dyhouse 1976). Furthermore, any attempt to educate women on a mass scale would prove, and indeed had already proved, damaging to such progress. Since the breeding of men lay with women, the education of women would detract from their essential function of breeding the future race. 'The deficiency of reproductive power amongst them', he argued, 'may be reasonably attributed to the overtaxing of their brains' (Spencer 1857, cited in Dyhouse 1976: 43). It could equally well be argued that the education of women was paramount if they are breeding men. But Spencer's kind of 'Darwinism' was firmly in line with conservative thought of the time. In short, sexism as well as racism could easily find a refuge in the application of evolutionary ideas to human society.

Progress therefore consisted of keeping the human stock as

healthy and productive as possible. In this respect, however, there was a clear distinction between Spencer's and Darwin's 'social Darwinism'. Spencer, like most 'Darwinian' writers in the nineteenth century, was very much more reliant than Darwin (and especially the Darwin of *The Origin*) on the notion that acquired characteristics would be biologically transmitted to the next generation (Bowler 1988). In other words, Spencer had no idea until reading Darwin and Wallace that variations were actively (and randomly) produced in the process of natural selection. This was a major flaw or gap in his thinking which he later acknowledged in his *Autobiography* (Spencer 1904: 501–2).

As regards social structure, transition from an unstructured homogeneity to a structured heterogeneity is made the core theme in Spencer's understanding of social evolution. And at this stage we can see the key connections he made between evolution in the physical and natural spheres on the one hand and in the social sphere on the other. He saw homogeneity as incoherent and unstable not just in the physical and natural spheres but also in the human social sphere. A homogenous structure, whether in the social or natural sphere, consists of structures and functions which could not prevail as society, a type of organism, continued to grow. The tendency is again towards differentiation, with the separated and distinct parts increasingly reliant upon, and communicating with, each other. The parallels between animals and social life are, for Spencer, striking:

> A low animal, or the embryo of a high one, has few distinguishable parts; but along with its acquirement of greater mass, its parts multiply and simultaneously differentiate. It is thus with society. At first the unlikenesses among its groups are inconspicuous in number and degree; but as it becomes more populous, divisions and sub-divisions become more numerous and decided.
>
> (Spencer 1893: 437)

The discussion perhaps foreshadows ecological arguments of our own day in which biodiversity is seen as contributing to the stability and robustness of ecosystems.

Change, then, brought increasing complexity, with societies, like organisms, starting as small aggregations (with simple structures with little interdependence between their parts) and becoming highly differentiated into social classes trading goods and commodities. Even here Spencer maintains the organic analogy, with bloodstreams and veins being compared to goods and roads. Similarly, he makes analogies between the rise of government and the emergence of complex brains in mammals and in particular, of course, human beings. In these ways, change in human societies became 'naturalized', but as part of a wider natural and cosmic process also affecting the whole of humanity.

Important to Spencer's analysis is the distinction between simple and compounded societies. 'Simple' societies are those made of single, autonomous and homogeneous units. 'Compound' societies are those in which increasing heterogeneity is emerging. A supreme leader may now, for example, be ruling over a number of groups which have coalesced, by either force or mutual agreement. 'Doubly' and 'trebly compounded' societies are those made up by further integration of previously quite independent social units, the final version being that recognized in modern society as well as some older social forms such as the Roman Empire.

More specifically still, Spencer made the distinction between militant and industrial societies, with the tendency being a shift from the former to the latter. Militant societies, according to his typology, are characterized by an extreme centralization of power, with people compelled and disciplined into supporting such power. Industrial societies are characterized by the dispersal of power, by democracy, with governments working to support the individual rather than vice versa. Nevertheless, he saw in his own time an unwelcome return to elements of the old 'militant' society. He was deeply suspicious of, for example, the rise in the number of military expeditions being announced by the British Parliament and, interestingly, the rise of new forms of state intervention such as the Local Government Board. These entailed a recentralization of modern society, often orchestrated by ex-military personnel.

Spencer had a clear vision as to the perfect form of society. It was one in which individuals had the liberty to fully realize their potential, so long as they were not affecting the liberty of others. A long evolutionary process, one in which those individuals, families and races who did not adapt died out, would in the long run lead to a condition of a happiness for all. In an argument which prefigures some contemporary neo-liberal thought, Spencer actively supported what he called 'private beneficence', spontaneous forms of welfare given by individuals and groups to one another (Offer 1999). Such relationships remained in tune with his evolutionary

thinking. But he believed strongly that it was a mistake for governments to intervene in a winnowing process in which the 'fittest' sur-
vived and eventually self-fulfilment would extend right down to the
individual. Free trade, a free press and universal suffrage were to
be welcomed towards these ends and, unlike Darwin, Spencer had
no Malthusian fear of the effects of population growth. One of the
distinct capacities of the human species is that of adapting to changing circumstances. High birth rates would lead not only to a (welcomed) elimination of those who could not adapt to the new form
of social order but also to a new type of human being, one with new
capacities, including the capacity to cooperate with others.

Like other social evolutionists, Spencer therefore incorporated
some quite explicit notions of direction and progress. But while it
is very tempting to suggest that he saw his own society of late nine-
teenth- and early twentieth-century England as the ideal towards
which history had all along been developing, he does in fact briefly
mention a still 'higher' form of society, one in which intellectual and
aesthetic issues take precedence over the materialism of his own
society (Perrin 1976).

Spencer's work has been widely outlined and analysed. So too
has the influence of his analysis and politics on different societies
and classes (see, for example, Hofstadter 1959; Bannister 1979;
Hawkins 1997). As might be expected, the conservative or free-
market version of Darwinism and of Spencer's 'social Darwinism'
found greatest acceptance in the United States, the home of liberal
capitalism. But the extent and form of such take-up are subject to
some debate. The conservative thinker William Sumner is often
seen as the main proponent of social Darwinism in America. His
best-known view is that the struggle for survival is a central feature
of social life and that if some individuals fall by the wayside, then
that should not be a matter of regret. As people adjust themselves
in the contest against nature, great hardships will be endured. But

> we cannot blame our fellow-men for our share of these. My neighbour
> and I are both struggling to free ourselves from these ills. The fact that
> my neighbour has succeeded in this struggle better than I constitutes
> no grievance for me.
>
>   (Cited in Hofstadter 1959: 56)

On the other hand, Bannister argues that later liberal social
scientists in the United States have overestimated the significance

of conservative interpretations given to Spencer and Darwinism. Such overestimation helped to emphasize the extent to which liberals later moved away from ultra-conservatism but, Banister suggests, it is unfair to the original adaptations of Spencer's theory. In fact, Sumner himself eventually came to see social Darwinism as implying the need for social reform rather than the continuance of a bare-knuckle 'survival of the fittest'. Similarly, in European countries Darwin's message that human beings are essentially mutualistic and solidaristic creatures received special emphasis. This was the position particularly adopted by French anarchist thinkers such as Gautier and by Kropotkin, whom we will discuss later.

Social evolution: direction, progress and regress

In November 1858 Spencer sent a copy of his essays to Darwin (see Spencer 1996). They included a version of his general theory of the shift from homogeneity to heterogeneity. The argument again was that this process applied not just to the natural world but also to the social world. In early societies, for example, 'every man is a warrior, hunter, fisherman, tool-maker, builder, every woman performs the same drudgeries' (Spencer 1996: 19). Darwin's reaction was nothing if not discreet (Box 3). While he praises Spencer, it is clear that

---

Box 3   Letter from Charles Darwin to Herbert Spencer, 25 November 1858

Dear Sir,

I beg permission to thank you sincerely for your very kind present of your Essays. I have already read several of them with great interest. . . . I am at present preparing an abstract of a larger work on the changes of species; but I treat the subject simply as a naturalist & not from a general point of view; otherwise, in my opinion, your argument could not have been improved on & might have been quoted by me with great advantage. . . .

I beg leave to remain / Dear Sir / Yours truly obliged / C. Darwin

Source: Burkhardt (1996: 196). Reproduced with kind permission of Cambridge University Press.

he has no wish to similarly generalize his theory to society from nature.

But as evolutionary thought in the social sciences developed in the late nineteenth and early twentieth centuries it drew increasingly far away from the thinking of Darwin and the natural sciences. To a growing extent the idea of evolution was used as a metaphor, having little to do with evolutionary biology while not attempting the type of massive synthesis of the physical, natural and social sciences developed by Spencer. Furthermore, social scientists and scientists alike increasingly lifted and developed those parts of Darwin which they found familiar and acceptable and left those parts which they did not. Specifically, they placed particular emphasis on evolution as a purposeful and guided process. And, as Lamarck suggested, it was one in which individuals acquired the characteristics developed by their forebears. Bowler's (1988: 56) comment on natural scientists applies even more to social Darwinists such as Spencer: 'The majority of naturalists wanted not haphazard divergence but all-embracing regularities that would confirm their feeling that the world is the product of a rational plan of creation.' The result was a wide array of 'social Darwinisms'. Some of the themes we have detected earlier remained, while others joined them. In particular, the notion of a general direction to social change was retained. There nevertheless emerged different views on whether this direction was beneficial or detrimental to the social order.

Marx and Engels are representatives of the first tendency. They were in many respects critical of Darwin. Engels, for example, saw Darwinian theory as 'simply the transference from society to organic nature of Hobbes' theory of the war of each against all' (cited in Woods and Grant 1995: 321). Nevertheless, both Marx and Engels admired Darwin's work and saw their science of human history eventually being built on Darwin's ideas (Woods and Grant 1995). Most important from our viewpoint, however, they also divided world history into a series of evolutionary 'stages'. In *The German Ideology*, for example, they argue that European history has passed through four distinct eras: the communal or tribal; the ancient or classical; the feudal; and the capitalist (Marx and Engels 1970: 39–57). In *Capital* the earliest 'Asiatic' mode was added and in *Grundrisse* (Marx 1973: 47–514) Marx developed this scheme still further. Each society contained within it the basis of the next.

The social relations of one society had their origins in the preceding social formation or, to use a biological metaphor employed by Engels (1989: 274), 'the feudal Middle Ages developed in its womb the class which was destined in the future of the modern demand for equality: the bourgeoisie'. Similarly, capitalism contains in its midst elements of the future classless socialism (Elson 1979; Ramsey and Howarth 1984). Such a view has similarities with contemporary social movements such as 'prefigurative socialism' (Rowbotham *et al.* 1979).

We should note that Marx and Engels's stagism also applied to human societies' relations with nature. In *Grundrisse*, for example, there is a somewhat schematic argument to the effect that human social evolution was linked with the progressive alienation of people from nature. Early stages of society were characterized by forms of communal and collective ownership of land. These became denied under capitalism, with the result that the human species lost direct association with nature (Dickens 1996). Marx and Engels were therefore making important, if by no means clearly worked-out, connections between external nature, internal nature and social relations. While the stagism of Marx and Engels's work is suspect, they offer important clues for linking evolutionary and sociological thought. These will also be returned to later.

With Marx and Engels we find a paradoxical meeting with Spencer. Social evolution was developing, in an almost inevitable way, towards a final, climactic and perfect state. But not all social theorists remained sanguine about eventual outcomes. One of the big themes of nineteenth- and early twentieth-century social thought is of course the collapse of a society based on community. This therefore entailed recognizing a long-term direction but not one to be greatly welcomed.

Toennies (1955) is perhaps the most obvious example of this view. As is well known, he argued that the development of European society has been from unions of *Gemeinschaft* to associations of *Gemeinschaft* and from there to associations of *Gesellschaft* and, eventually, unions of *Gesellschaft*. He saw the archetypal unit of *Gemeinschaft* as the family and, mediated through the family, social union based on blood, land, kinship and neighbourhood. The final stage, unions of *Gesellschaft*, represented an attempted recovery of old forms of *Gemeinschaft*. Techniques of human relations, social security and job insurance created new aggregations of people which, superficially at least, resembled the old social order. But to the extent that these new unions are successful, this is so despite the disorganizing, individualizing and separating processes which are central to the new social order.

For Toennies, and for many other theorists of contemporary social change, therefore, social evolution has a definite direction but it is one in which evolution does not necessarily entail progress. An exception is Durkheim. According to Catton (1998), he read Darwin's theory inaccurately to imply that increasing diversity and speciation eventually lead to cooperation and mutualism rather than competition. The shift from a 'mechanical' type of solidarity (one based on tradition and the small community) to an 'organic' form of society based on the division of labour and the growth of individuality would bring increasing levels of cooperation. Such interpretation arose, Catton (1998: 106) suggests, because Durkheim 'ardently wanted to believe the past troubles in his native France were a prelude to a progressive future'.

But now, however, we are moving into the realm of the evolution as metaphor. There is little real contact with Darwin and scientific theories of biological evolution. Toennies alludes to the notion of intimate relations between people and land in earlier societies. But there is decreasing connection in these theories to natural selection in relation to an 'environment' within which human beings and their society are evolving.

Conclusion: social Darwinism and problems of methodology

Less discussed than the influences of Darwin, Spencer and evolutionary concepts on social thought are the often highly problematic methodological tensions in social Darwinism and in Spencer in particular. At many points, including his notion of a cosmic evolutionary process influencing all processes and organisms on earth, he is maintaining that human society is obeying the same laws as are affecting the natural world. He is attempting map out a single science, an enterprise which Marx and, to a greater degree, Engels had already attempted.

However, Spencer inadequately specified the complex relationships between human society, evolutionary and ecological processes and physical laws. Contemporary realist epistemology now recognizes, for example, that there are distinct relationships and causal processes operating within each of these spheres (for an extended discussion, see Collier 1994). The physical world has its own causal powers within which the biological, ecological and social worlds must operate. Similarly, there are distinct evolutionary and developmental processes in the natural world within which human society must develop. Finally, human society is of course subject to these processes and laws but is not determined by them. There are real causal mechanisms and processes, such as class relations, which form a distinct feature of human society and social change. But instead of attempting such a stratified view of the world, and one which recognizes the causal mechanisms operating within each strata, Spencer adopted a cosmic overview of evolutionary processes and proceeded to squeeze the whole of human social life within it. This picture specified the relations between human society and nature in a form which was simple and perhaps persuasive. But in the end it was highly misleading.

There are further important theoretical and epistemological issues here. Evolutionary ideas, whether of a Spencerian or a directly Darwinian nature, were very much a 'social construction'. And such ideas became recruited to serve distinct social and political interests. Darwin's scientific ideas were also a product of his time. As we have seen, this is a point made by Engels. It was also made by Marx when he wrote to Engels that 'it is remarkable how Darwin recognises in beasts and plants his English society with its divisions of labour, competition, opening up of new markets, "inventions" and the Malthusian "struggle for existence"' (quoted in Schmidt 1971: 46). But Marx and Engels were also sufficiently gracious to say that even though Darwin's ideas were a product of his time they were by and large correct and would eventually prove to be the basis of a general social theory.

Thus although Darwin's theory was, in modern terms, a 'social construction', it was much more than that. It claimed to describe real processes, specifically those of blind variation and selection, which (combined with sexual selection and a shortage of resources) actually exist in the real world of nature. And, to the extent to which Darwin's theory has stood the test of time, it can indeed claim to have discovered some of the key underlying mechanisms in the natural and human spheres. But how these mechanisms relate to the human social world is one of the great challenges to social theorists and natural scientists alike. The project of developing a social science which draws from the natural and physical sciences but which adequately incorporates what is specific to human society is an extremely difficult, not to say over-ambitious, undertaking. One way in which it can be attempted is sketched out later.

2

Evolutionary Thought in Contemporary Sociology

The previous chapter identified three closely linked themes in evolutionary thought, particularly as it has been applied to social change. These are progress occurring through evolution, direction to social change and teleology, an end which is built into social change itself. These continue to inform contemporary social theory. As this chapter will suggest, however, such an inheritance is proving highly problematic.

The Darwinian concept of evolution carried no presumption that change necessarily entailed progress or direction. The future is seen as open, and the direction of change is contingent. Nor, despite Darwin's occasional suggestions to the contrary, does the theory imply any notion of 'direction' or inbuilt 'end'. Darwin's whole theory was based on the whole idea of spontaneous variation occurring in organic species. This means that increasing complexity and heterogeneity in nature are not necessary outcomes. Mutation is random, as is environmental change. A direction towards complexity or heterogeneity would necessitate some underlying cause or deity monitoring the interactions between organism and environment. No such causal mechanism or deity is known to exist (Hirst 1976). Modern ecological theory suggests that complexity (in, for example, the form of a 'climax community') is more stable, but this does not imply 'direction' as such.

The supposed direction towards greater complexity or hetero-geneity is problematic in another sense. If, for example, organisms were analysed at the molecular level rather than at the level of brain, heart and lungs, the notion of 'increasing complexity' or 'increasing heterogeneity' would again be difficult to maintain.

Neither Darwin nor modern genetically-based biology therefore provides any real support for notions of progress, direction and teleology. Yet these notions still loom very large in modern social thought. And a great deal of this thinking has some notion of social evolution built into it. Some examples follow. Arguments over whether social change has resulted in 'progress', whether there is a 'direction' to social development and whether there is some kind of 'end' contained within social change have become conflated with evolutionary thinking. To put this another way, there is plenty of scope for argument about social change and whether it exhibits some broad patterns. But this has rather little to do with evolution as understood by the natural sciences. However, despite this funda-mental failing, some legacies from older social theory can be used in constructing an improved approach.

Social evolution and the achievement of progress

Perhaps the best-known example of an emergent progress associ-ated with modernity was in modernization theory, an area of work which now, it must be said, commands little support (Lerner 1958; Rostow 1960). A fully developed society, it was argued, relied on the existence of a particular set of modern institutions. These included a value system supportive of economic growth, but it also rested on a 'modern' set of educational, political, legal and edu-cational systems. 'Traditional' societies are those whose social structure 'is developed within limited production functions, based on pre-Newtonian science and technology, and on pre-Newtonian attitudes towards the physical world' (Rostow 1960: 4) Such sys-tems had to be disposed of if economic development was to occur. Clan-based or autocratic forms of government were an obstacle, as were certain forms of education, custom and tradition such as the 'pre-Newtonian attitudes' mentioned above. Dispensing with such institutions (or, to put the matter more passively, 'the passing of traditional society') was therefore seen as an essential prerequisite for 'take-off'. One way in which this was to be achieved was through culture, through an educated vanguard driving modernization forward. Prerequisites for take-off also included the application of new technologies and capital investments to the land and natural resources of traditional society:

> It is therefore an essential condition for a successful transition that investment be increased and – even more important – that the hitherto unexploited back-log of innovations be brought to bear on a society's land and other natural resources, where quick increases in output are possible.
>
> (Rostow 1960: 22)

Almost inevitably, a picture envisaging a series of development stages finishes by placing societies on a spectrum. African tribes or Australian aborigines would find themselves placed at one end of the spectrum, having had the ill luck not to be invested in and hence not having progressed. Nevertheless, there was always the possibility that they could be economically upgraded. Meanwhile others, such as the United States or western Europe, are located at the other, most modern end. Such thinking in large part echoed nineteenth-century evolutionary thought, previously 'backward' societies now being called 'traditional'.

It now seems unsurprising that this type of neo-evolutionary thinking ran into many difficulties. First, those who attempted to use such theorizing found it very difficult to do so. There are, for example, severe problems in measuring the central characteristics of modernization. The presence of economic investment in a 'traditional' society tells us very little about what that investment was used for. Was it to improve the conditions of the people living there or was it to provide raw materials and resources for the richer, already modern, societies? Again, it is not necessarily clear that even if 'traditional' societies did adopt modern institutions (such as large bureaucracies) such innovations would necessarily lead to substantial economic development. The criticisms of this view which in the end proved most telling were those of Frank (1972). He dismissed the whole basis for such thinking about social evolution. The idea of 'stages', he believed, was completely unconvincing on historical grounds. It is unconvincing, he believed, not least because not all societies experience the same sequence. In no way, for example, do

'Third World' societies now resemble the conditions from which now-developed countries once emerged. Underdeveloped Third World societies, he argued, were subjected to intensive colonial domination by both Europe and the United States. Whether or not a society remained 'traditional' or 'modern' had little to do with its internal characteristics and everything to do with whether it held 'satellite status' relative to now-developed societies:

> Historical research demonstrates that contemporary underdevelopment is in large part the historical product of past and continuing economic and other relations between the satellite underdeveloped and the now developed metropolitan countries.
>
> (Frank 1972: 3)

The debates continue. In particular, neo-liberal theorists and even some Marxists now argue that Frank and others were too wholesale and unsubtle in their criticisms of modernization theory. Asia is pointed to as successful precisely because it opened up to Western culture and technology and industrial methods. Colonization is now seen as bringing gains as well as disbenefits. As Saunders (1995: 34) puts it on behalf of the neo-liberals, '[f]or all its harshness and unfairness, . . . the net effects of colonization for economic development have arguably been more beneficial than harmful'. World living standards have increased, as have health levels in all parts of the world. Such debates are not, however, the central point of this text. What has been thoroughly forgotten in such arguments is the whole concept of 'evolution' as understood by the natural sciences. 'Stagism' and other evolutionary ideas borrowed and adapted from natural science by social and political theorists have not only made little real contact with evolutionary theory, it is at least arguable that the application of evolutionary thought to the social world has been obfuscatory. Through neglecting both internal and external nature, they have finished up reinforcing the culture–nature divide which has long bedevilled Western thought. Before considering how evolutionary thought can be brought back into the picture, we need to turn to the other two themes central to evolutionary thought in the social sciences.

A direction to social evolution?

Another closely related theme in the social evolution literature is the idea of societies, and indeed all societies, progressing through a series of stages or sequences. We find it in much sociological think-ing: the supposed transition from a 'modern' society to a 'post-modern' society or from a modern to a 'late modern' social order. All this is, at base, another borrowing from nineteenth-century social thought. In particular, it is a close cousin of Herbert Spencer's thinking about 'structural differentiation'. As we have seen, his suggestion was that evolution of all kinds (including social evolution) entails the transition from simple, homogeneous struc-tures to complex heterogeneous structures defined by increasing levels of specialization. The continuing stagism of social thought has been very pervasive. As we have also seen, it formed part of Marx's thinking and it was a central part of Toennies theory of a growing individualism, competition and impersonality followed by a partial recovery of older forms of community.

Given today's environmental consciousness, a particularly intriguing version of the 'directionalism' thesis comes from anthro-pology, specifically from Steward's 'cultural ecology'. This is one of the few occasions when ecological considerations have been sys-tematically built into the social theory. Steward (1955: 36, cited in Sanderson 1990) argued that inclusion of environmental consider-ations overcomes 'the fruitless assumption that culture comes from culture' (see also Sanderson 1994). He suggested a similar direction to early social evolution. Drawing on archaeological data, he argued that in Mesopotamia, Egypt, India, China and Peru there had been similar transitions from hunter-gatherer societies to an increasingly intensive agriculture and eventually towards militaris-tic and empire-building regimes and increasingly rigid class struc-tures. In all this he posits two-way processes between societies and their ecological contexts. Extensive political control was needed to create the irrigation systems needed for farming. But intensified agriculture resulted in population growth which created conflicts and war within these societies. These conflicts in turn led to further conquests and empire building. The result was further militarism and concentration of class power and further attempts to control natural resources through irrigation.

Ecological considerations received some consideration in the work of one of the best-known twentieth-century exponents of evo-lutionary thought in the social sciences, Talcott Parsons. To under-stand his approach to social evolution we must first understand that he believed functioning systems of all kinds, from the scale of

society to that of personality, possessed certain underlying properties. These are:

(A) Adaptation to their environment. A social system, for ex-
    ample, must obtain and distribute resources necessary for its
    survival and development.
(G) A definition of goals and the mobilization of effort and energy
    into achieving them. A social system must, for example,
    identify its goals and motivate actors into achieving them.
(I) The integration and coordination of parts. For a society to func-
    tion properly, for example, social cohesion must be maintained.
(L) The maintenance of latency or pattern maintenance. A soci-
    ety, for example, must store and distribute ideas and symbols.
    These are essential for the management of a society and its
    social tensions.

Parsons also theorized the relations between subsystems, in particular between biological, personality, social and cultural systems.
In general, he believed that 'high-information' subsystems control
'high-energy' subsystems. Thus organisms supply energy to the personality (or psychological) system, the personality system supplies
energy to the social system and the social system supplies energy
(through people's roles) to the cultural system of values. But it is
the cultural system which ultimately dominates the whole social
system. It supplies information to the social system, the social
system supplies information to the personality system, and the personality system supplies information to the biological organism. In
summary, it is the complete opposite to Marx, culture as dominating biology, personality and society, rather than the economy dominating cultural and other aspects of social life.

Social evolution, according to Parsons, has gone through three
stages. The 'primitive' stage was that in which writing stabilized
culture across time. The 'intermediate' stage was that in which rules
of law institutionalized ideals and codified norms and customs.
Finally, 'modern' societies are those in which mass education and
the rise of professional classes have transformed the cultural
system. Note again the continuing importance of culture as dominating all aspects of social change. Parsons recognized that causes
of change in the social system can be generated by external pres-
sures, such as environmental change. But they can also be a result
of endogenous systems, such as strain in the family 'subsystem'.

Parsons promoted a general law of all forms of evolution, social as well as biological. Note the similarities with Spencer at this point. Parsons believed that evolutionary change generally entails the increasing differentiation of parts on the one hand and the establishment of new forms of integration on the other. So as societies change through time we can, he believed, see the differentiation of systems from each other. For example, the extended family withdraws from its economic functions in early industrialization and specializes in the socializing of children. Further differentiation takes place within the family. Males go out and earn money to raise families, while females specialize in socialization and general child care. Each increasingly differentiated subsystem (for example, the factory and the home) becomes improved in terms of its adaptive capacity, or its capacity to survive.

But as each new differentiation comes into being, society must be more adaptive, it must be able to better cope with the problems with which it is faced. As the process of differentiation continues, Parsons envisages the emergence of new problems of coordination. New skills and abilities are needed and this entails incorporating more people as active members of society, using and realizing their potentials. The value system of a society undergoing these changes must itself undergo change. On the one hand increasing differentiation means that it is difficult to find a value system which can encompass everyone. Assuming society is not going to fly apart as it becomes increasingly diversified, a new and still more generalized set of values must be created which attempts to incorporate all members of society. The most important development in the transition from intermediate to modern was the creation of modern law, or what he called 'the institutionalised codes of normative order' (Parsons 1966: 26).

Parsons's evolutionary model is in many ways very challenging. He remains one of the few modern sociologists to have taken the external environment and the biologically evolved organism at all seriously. The 'adaptive function' of systems, he suggested, is the means by which links are made between society and environment. Furthermore, the (highly flexible) human organism is the means by which this adaptation takes place. His pioneering attempt to link biological, evolutionary and social systems has become largely lost by later social theory.

Criticisms of Parsons have been very considerable. His modern society, for example, looks very like the United States of America. The implication is that this is the end to which all societies will necessarily be evolving. The forms of 'differentiation' seem to deny forms of agency. Feminism, for example, has recently said and done much about recent 'differentiation' within the family 'subsystem'. More generally, the very high levels of abstraction at which he operated cry out for much precise explication of the mechanisms involved. By insisting on 'properties of subsystems' he ends up telling us rather little, for example, about how organisms develop in relation to their environment. He tells us very little about the varying and changing ways in which human societies actually interact with and are influenced by the causal powers of nature. In short, 'systems' are reified or given a life of their own at the expense of understanding the actual mechanisms involved. Parsons therefore began to define the scope of a new liaison between evolutionary and social thought, but he did not adequately clarify how the complexities of this liaison should be conceptualized.

Smelser (1959) was another evolutionist with similarities to Parsons. He argued that in traditional societies the full range of necessary functions was carried out within single structures such as families, kinship networks or tribes. Social evolution, however, involves these functions being undertaken by specialist structures. An increasingly complex society evolves with, for example, work taking place in factories, education in schools, health care in hospitals. Like Spencer as well as Parsons, therefore, Smelser was again pointing to increased differentiation in society. Such differentiation again, however, brought potential problems. Differentiation and increasing specialization were all very well, but they also needed integration. Those societies which do not achieve integration are likely to experience serious problems.

Unlike many functionalist sociologists, Smelser (1959) attempted to apply his ideas. His theory echoes that of Spencer and Parsons. But as the quotation in Box 4 suggests, increasing differentiation was part of a general move towards social 'progress'. One element in his picture of 'growth', 'advancement' and 'civilization' is that the social structures in question become more differentiated from each other.

Writers such as Parsons and Smelser, like those implying a sense of 'progress' to social change, have also come under severe attack. Again, this is largely because the notion of a general and underlying sense of evolution to social change contained a strong implication

Box 4 Social evolution in functionalist sociology: Smelser's study of early industrialism

Smelser used case-study material from the Lancashire cotton industry during the period of early industrialization in the late eighteenth century. Work became increasingly specialized around certain tasks. Increasingly, work that was previously in 'cottage industry' form was was taken into factories. But even in these new workplaces there arose new problems of coordination. But impacts on the home were also considerable. As work began to take place elsewhere there arose a need for new institutions which could provide alternatives to the previously close-knit home. New kinds of organization such as savings banks, cooperative societies and trade unions developed. Again, the picture is one of increasing specialization. And such specialization was still further increased as there arose a need for new legal institutions to adequately regulate and link these developing institutions. The general picture offered by Smelser is one of seven stages. In the first stage dissatisfaction is expressed with some feature of the social system such as the use of resources. In Smelser's next five stages this dissatisfaction is dealt with. In the final stage, and 'after a period of extraordinary progress' (Smelser 1959: 402), society is reintegrated, but in a much more differentiated form as new, more specialized institutions emerge and become an established part of the social system.

that the ultimate form of development for all societies is indeed the Western world. And again, it was writers like Frank (1972) working from a broadly Marxist perspective (themselves now considered to be somewhat outdated) who brought about the eventual downfall of this type of evolutionary thinking. Smelser's empirical work on the undermining of the home and the rise of the factory contained valuable insights but the phenomena he examined are more easily understood by using terms such as capitalism, the division of labour and proletarianization than differentiation, functions, subsystems and so forth. (Indeed, it might be interesting to rework Smelser's empirical work using alternative concepts borrowed from historical materialism and political economy.) Again, however, Marxist dismissals of this kind of evolutionary thinking are not the key concern here. There are still more important matters.

First there is the matter of 'differentiation', one which applied to

Spencer, of course, as well as Parsons. The analogy between differentiation in the natural and the social worlds is a pervasive one.
As we have seen, however, even in the biological sphere it is difficult to assert a law of differentiation. The issue hangs crucially on
which scale of analysis is being used. Similarly, it is unclear in either
Spencer's or Parson's work at what level 'differentiation' of the
social structure is supposed to be taking place. At one moment it is
the individual, at another the nation, at yet another a race. At the
same time, the dismissal of evolutionary thought of the kind
mounted by Frank has also led to the wholesale and completely
unsatisfactory rejection of any kind of link between evolutionary
thought and social theory. A remedy must be found, one which
holds on to the useful insights of these evolutionists, but one which
better explicates the connections between social development and
evolutionary change.

Social evolution as teleological?

A final theme in evolutionary thought as applied to human society
is the notion that evolution is developing towards some 'end'. Perhaps the nearest to such a proposition in the contemporary literature comes from some environmental philosophers. Matthews and
some 'deep greens', for example, argue that the universe as a whole
and elements within it such as ecological systems, organisms
(including human beings) and even inorganic objects have an
intrinsic value (Matthews 1991; Naess 1989). Full realization of such
value will come about when human society creates a new set of
environmentally grounded values. Environmental philosophy of
this kind, however, runs into major difficulties. Given the complexity of human society's relations with the environment and the competition between species over resources, how can new ecologically
sound values be realistically envisaged? (See Hayward 1998.) What
really is the end – or, more precisely, the diverse and sometimes
conflicting ends – towards which both people and nature are
developing and eventally evolving? Who or what could determine
such ends? A large part of the problem stems from the profound
neglect of social and power relations in this type of environmental
philosophy. But when we turn to social theory we find a mirror
image. It largely neglects the environment.

There are few if any social theorists now who would argue, in a quasi-religious way, that society is unfolding towards an end that was always intended. Its modern version takes the form of an assumed and ever-present logic to social evolution, even if the end was never entirely predictable. One of its most recent versions, one which has some close links to Hegel's thought, is Fukuyama's (1992) famous assertion that liberal capitalism has now become almost universally endorsed as 'the end of history'. Liberal democratic capitalism has triumphed as a historical terminus because it has given every person a sense of recognition and worth, while at the same time providing high levels of material well-being. One implication is that history (driven by the development of science and technology) has all along been evolving towards this 'end'. Fukuyama has now, however, revised some of his assertions, and in ways which touch on some of our key concerns. On the one hand he argues that humans have a 'natural capacity for solving problems of social cooperation and inventing rules to constrain individual choice' (Fukuyama 1999a: 231). This capacity will, in the long run, counter social malaise, high crime-levels and societal breakdown. A relatively harmonious 'end' to social development is therefore in sight, a product of our genetic inheritance. But in a way that encapsulates many current confusions about the importance of human genes, he also suggests that biotechnology will shortly allow humans to take charge of their own evolution. According to this view, humans as such will have been 'abolished' by genetic manipulation and a new 'post human' history will have commenced. Either way, Fukuyama attributes much to human genetic structure both in understanding long-run social development and in 'ending' humanity. As we will later see, however, such faith in genes and 'human nature' is highly problematic.

An older version of the thesis that social direction is imposed by technological innovation was the 'convergence' thesis of such writers as Kerr *et al.* (1960) and Aron (1969). The argument was that the differences and distinctions between different forms of industrialization were of fairly minor import compared with their similarities and, more particularly, with the underlying causes of these similarities. A modern industrial based society, whether capitalist or communist, commits its people to the drive for economic growth and the development of efficient management towards this end. In particular, industrialism's demands on technology and science in turn mean that '[t]he industrial system requires a wide range of skills and professional competency broadly distributed throughout the workforce' (Kerr *et al.* 1960: 34–5).

Similarly, the function of the extended family is undermined. Education takes place through specialist institutions, and indeed the extended family falls apart as a result of industrialism's general need for mobility. The work ethic thrives, leading states and voluntary organizations to provide functions previously undertaken by the family. This in turn generates laws to regulate and link the new institutions. In these ways societies undergo forms of *re*-integration. Communism is seen as just one form of industrialization, one way in which an industrial society becomes embarked on. Similarly, the managerial and political elites of a communist or capitalist society will, whatever their original objectives, eventually adapt their thinking to the imperatives of a technologically-driven industrial society.

A related argument came with the so-called 'post-industrial' thesis. Again, the implication is that economic production imposes an underlying and homogenizing order on all societies. There were at least three versions of this argument, all of them positing not only a notion of an underlying mechanism to social evolution but also a distinct and universal progression from one kind of society to another. Touraine *et al.* (1965) and Mallet (1975) envisaged a shift from a society based on the production of things to one based on the production of knowledge. They envisaged a growing division between those who are highly educated and those who are not. On the one hand there will be a new class of highly educated people, and on the other an older working class. This, they argued, was a recipe for social chaos and disorder. We will encounter new versions of this thesis later in this study.

Mann (1973) envisaged social evolution typically going through three 'phases', with technology and changes in the labour process providing the underlying motor for change. Although Mann rejected much of Marx (and, in particular, Marx's faith in the revolutionary potential of the working class) there remain some strong links here with the stages and the mechanisms underlying human alienation which underpinned Marx's historical materialism. As discussed later, this type of analysis can be usefully carried through into a modern synthesis of evolutionary and social-scientific thought. 'Phase A' in Mann's analysis is based on small-scale craft production, and fulfilment based on the potential for workers to make use of their particular skills. 'Phase B' is based on standard-ization, large orders, a homogeneous workforce and jobs which are 'intrinsically alienating' (Mann 1973: 54). 'Phase C' entails increas-ing 'technological progress', continuous production, with the worker being made into 'purely a machine minder'. Nevertheless, according to Mann (and it is at this point that he parts company with Marx) there are prospects for emancipation in this most recent stage of capitalism. An element of collective, group working is introduced and freedom of movement is allowed. Furthermore, a reskilling process starts to be put in place: 'The worker has to develop new skills in order to look after such complex and expen-sive machinery successfully, and so job satisfaction rises again' (Mann 1973: 55).

Another more optimistic version of 'post-industrial' thesis was that advanced by Bell (1973). It argued that the 'advanced' Western societies are now undergoing a qualitative change, or a new stage, in their development. The creation and spread of knowledge is the key mechanism here. We live, it is argued, in an era in which know-ledge becomes a key resource, with a special premium being placed on technical experts. These experts are becoming the dominant social class, taking over from old-style industrialists. They are the highly educated people with the knowledge of science and tech-nology which has so far escaped the original captains of industry. Another feature of the post-industrial landscape is the rise of service industry alongside the industries making goods and the rise of white-collar workers alongside blue-collar operatives. Again, this is all part of a new kind of society in which knowledge sup-posedly supplants things as the key item consumers wish to buy.

Convergence theory and 'post-industrial' theory therefore implicitly contained a sense of an inbuilt and technological logic to society; one which laid down the basic ground-rules for social change as a whole and for all developing societies. For many of these authors there was a sense in which society was inevitably being taken in a certain direction. Such a direction was largely a result of mechanisms contained within society – technology, for example, or science and knowledge. Similarly, a particular class of people within society were attributed immense powers relative to the rest of the population.

This type of thinking by social scientists, like the others we have considered earlier, has now largely dropped explicit reference to evolution. Nevertheless, the idea of a *deus ex machina*, a generating force taking society in a certain direction, still haunts social theory. The transition from modernity to 'postmodernity' or to a 'risk society' is a case in point (Beck 1992). And as we have seen, a notion of an inbuilt direction is alive and well in Fukuyama's work. On the other hand, there are many reasons for rejecting this view. Future forms of social evolution can be considered just as open and unpredictable as those in the natural world. For example, capitalism could lead to demands for a new sense of personal recognition, one in which workers could recognize they are capable of controlling production processes for themselves (Chitty 1994). This again suggests, *inter alia*, that concepts of 'endism', direction and so forth may be making too many assumptions about human nature. Humans, as we will discuss later, are active, reflexive and flexible, and this alone should lead to great caution regarding theories about long-term historical trends. Again, the application of evolutionary thought to social theory has been in some ways helpful (pointing up, for example, emergent forms of social change) while in other ways it has proved highly obfuscatory. This is for two main reasons. First, it has uncritically assumed direction, purpose and progress to social evolution. Second, it has (with some important exceptions) neglected or taken for granted both internal and external nature.

Social evolution: contemporary work and ways forward

Critiques of evolutionary thought in the social sciences have led to evolutionary thought becoming largely frozen out by social theory (Sanderson 1990). The problem continues today. German social theory, in particular, has recently witnessed growth in evolutionary thought, sometimes fusing elements of Parsons with a dash of Marxism. There are differences within this group of sociologists but they, like Parsons, all retain a notion of society as a form of social organism. They also raise the question as to whether society has some form of inbuilt direction. Habermas is a case in point. He believes that social systems need what he calls 'a reflexive centre', one which accumulates knowledge of itself in a process of self-understanding. On the other hand, he believes that modern societies are increasingly disintegrating into 'specialized subsystems'. The result is an inbuilt tendency towards disorder:

None of the subsystems could occupy the top of a hierarchy and represent the whole the way the emperor could once do for the empire in stratified societies. Modern societies no longer have at their disposal an authoritative centre for self-reflection and steering.

(Habermas 1996: 357)

Similarly, Eder (1984, 1987) has a view of modern society as evolving as a collective learning system. But he places less stress on inbuilt steering problems associated with the fragmentation of society into subsystems. He argues that a moral code slowly develops as a way of resolving disputes and class struggles. We are part, he argues, of a learning society, one in which cultural evolution (involving human communication) takes place separately from biological evolution. Most recently, he has stressed the relative separation between human learning and social change (Eder 1999). The risks created by modern society, for example, lead to new bouts of knowledge creation. The learning society provides the context for social change ('the stuff out of which society selects its own continuous reproduction') but it does not directly determine the direction or form of such change.

Luhmann (1982, 1989) was another influential German sociologist for whom systems theory was important. Significantly, he was once a student of Parsons. Luhmann also argued that modern society is characterized by its continuing functional differentiation into what he calls 'autopoietic' subsystems. These are parts of the whole which have their own operating codes and rules to which they alone refer. This process has advantages and disadvantages. On the one hand people are liberated from the impositions of centralized and autocratic power. As regards the external environment:

systems with greater complexity are generally capable of entertaining more and different kinds of relations with their environments (for example, of separating inputs and outputs) and thus of reacting to an environment with greater complexity.

(Luhmann 1989: 12)

On the other hand, this fragmentation leads to each autopoietic system often producing external and detrimental effects with which other systems then have to cope. In this case, then, there is very little in the way of direction to social development. Modern societies are simultaneously creating and resolving problems on an *ad hoc* and unplanned basis. This again includes environmental degradation, where the communication problems deriving from separated subsystems are intense. This type of analysis links to Beck (1992), who refers to the 'organised irresponsibility' of modern society. He also argues that societal subsystems work according to their own codes. The economy works on being profitable, politics concentrates on winning the next election, science works on establishing the truth independent of how the science is used, while the legal system is hamstrung by the limitations of the laws it has created in the past. All this, Beck argues, leads to 'super-dangers' or a 'risk society', one again stemming from the increasing functional differentiation of society and a consequent inability to deal with the overarching problems it is creating.

Compared with earlier theorists such as Parsons, evolutionary thought is sometimes much less explicit in these recent developments. Furthermore, the history of evolutionary thought in the social sciences seems to have entailed an increasing distancing of social theory from biologism – that is, from the view that explanation can be gained by biological theory. But the analogies between biological and social evolution are still highly influential, as in the work of Luhmann and Eder. Again, there are many useful elements to these contemporary forms of systems thinking, particularly in terms of exploring the extent to which social development is associated with order or disorder. They introduce a welcome focus on humans and human groups as capable of a degree of *self*-evolution, their mental capacities giving them the capacity to learn and adapt to new circumstances.

The emphasis in this work on societies as interacting systems and on the increasing differentiation of functions means that these later German writers are in many respects the heirs to a line of social thought which started with Spencer and continued with Parsons. This in itself is not necessarily a problem, but questions must be raised over whether the analogies between biological evolution and social 'evolution' are really worthwhile. How, for example, is the biological notion of differentiation (as distinct from, say, the social and technical division of labour) really helping our understanding? What actually are the 'systems' which these authors use as their conceptual starting point? Is it really necessary, for example, to deploy systems theory and a latter-day Parsonianism or Spencerism to explore whether modern societies are more or less controllable?

Those using these concepts would answer that systems thinking is necessary in order to understand the connections between the parts. But when it comes to linking the actual parts (processes of biological evolution, their interaction with social relations and institutions, for example) surely the priority must again be that of specifying the actual causal mechanisms involved and their relations to the powers of both internal and external nature. Without doing so we can never know, for example, whether 'superdangers', 'risk societies' and indeed 'systems' are any more than a figment of the sociologist's imagination. In short, systems analysis and the analogy between biological and social systems may have generated valuable insights, but it remains doubtful whether the problems and issues now being addressed can in the end be adequately understood within the systems frameworks within which they started to be analysed.

This chapter has traced the move in social theory away from analogies between social change and evolution in nature. Traces of evolutionary thought remain, however, in systems theory. But the price of moving away from evolutionary thought has been the increasing denial of the relations between culture and nature. Some of these problems, particularly that of the relation between culture and *human* nature, will now be addressed.

3

Nature–Culture Dualism and Beyond

This chapter makes a first move towards a new link between evolutionary and social thinking. It first discusses some of the specific, and often unhelpful, ways in which evolutionary ideas are still being been built into social theory. While notions of social evolution have helped their disciplines to become somewhat more coherent, they are failing to incorporate any adequate understanding of people as a natural sort, one with an evolved history. In biology we find a reverse problem: theories of human society based on genetics turn out to have limited and inadequate understandings of society and social change. An integration entails exploring the links between society and humans as a natural sort. A key link between biological and cultural evolution is the making of human self-identity in a social context. Humans have an especially well-developed sense of self. Such sense of self is made in relation to society, formed by it and in turn helping to form social relations.

Western culture is largely premised on a split between humans on the one hand and nature on the other. This dualism can be traced at least as far back as the beginnings of the Judaeo-Christian tradition (Capra 1983; Ingold 1986). It became especially important in the seventeenth century with the rise of Descartes, Bacon and the beginnings of an industrial society. At this point the dualism was made into one between unequals, 'nature' being available as 'resources' as a means for developing human 'culture'. Despite the rise in environmental concerns, the dichotomy remains strongly evident in contemporary social and biological thought. On the one hand social scientists remain (with some important exceptions) largely oblivious or even hostile to the insights of the natural sciences (Benton 1991).

Meanwhile the natural sciences are prone to force social or cultural thought into their own framework of analysis.

Take, for example, evolutionary economics. Economists have long made analogies between the world of people and the world of nature. We have already found Marx and Spencer using biological metaphors for the understanding of change, albeit in very different ways and with very different prescriptions for reform. And as Hodgson (1993) has usefully shown, evolutionary ideas exercised a considerable and constant influence on twentieth-century economic thought. Authors as distinguished as Veblen, Schumpeter and Hayek all depended in different ways on insights from evolutionary thought. Contemporary evolutionary economics now appears to be a fast-growing field. They have shown that analogies can be feasibly made between advanced industrial economies and the workings of nature.

Since the pioneering work of Alchian, evolutionary economics has concentrated on the firm as its unit of analysis.(Alchian 1950; Nelson and Winter 1982). Rival companies are seen as making a range of products, with each adopting forms of technology, systems of organization and management practices. They are therefore seen as trying out in a 'blind', unconscious way (one analogous to the blind variations of genetics in the natural world) combinations of technical innovation and management routines which they hope will give competitive advantage in terms of quality and price. Again the process is seen as random, there being no long-term plan or guarantee of success. 'Natural selection' in the economy, according to this perspective, takes the form of those companies which do not make a profit going to the wall, with consumers meanwhile comparing prices and quality and buying accordingly. Conversely, those that are 'economically fit' are those which make successful combinations of technology and management practices to increase their market share and make the highest profits. Clearly, and despite the randomness involved, this process can be seen as more sophisticated and dynamic. A firm is able to observe another successful institution and copy its practices. It can observe and copy the new innovations of its competitors and thereby invade other companies' 'niches'. Yet this process contains the seeds of its own downfall. The process of economic evolution can in the long run lead to economic concentration and monopoly. If this happens, and if there are no new entrants into the process, the drive towards innovation may slow down, innovation may not continue and profits may decline.

Such analogies are suspect, even in their own terms. They remain couched at the economic level, failing to demonstrate how firms shape their own 'environment' through, for example, advertising and political lobbying. They have, however, done something to help economics confront questions of time, information and learning and thereby bring this particular discipline to something nearer the real world. They have also helped overcome the assumption of equilibrium in conventional economics, one in which supply and demand curves are the main focus and are seen as condensing or aggregating individual consumers' and producers' behaviour. As Junge (1993: 216) writes:

> To observe the economy as a system structured by evolutionary pro-
> cesses has the advantage of grasping more of the crucial aspects of
> economic life than most of the other equilibrium models could handle.
> Until recently this advantage could only be had at the price of verbal
> vagueness, but this is now compensated to an increasing degree by the
> building and testing of computer models aiming to simulate the sto-
> chastic processes of economic evolution.

But the price of avoiding such 'verbal vagueness' is to again fail to see the real and crucial connections between economics and the natural world. In the end evolutionary economics remains only analogy, and evolution itself is left out. Evolutionary economics fails to see either humans as themselves a product of evolution or the economy in relation to the 'resources' which it needs for further so-called 'evolution'. The 'environment' in these models remains simply the 'environment' of consumers and other competitors. The net result is that the dichotomy between culture and nature remains intact with little or no enlightenment regarding the relations between the two.

The position becomes more complex and unclear when we turn to other social sciences. Few contemporary social scientists now subscribe to the notions of teleology, progress and direction which were an implicit feature of nineteenth- and early twentieth-century writers. One of the most distinguished examples of opposition to such claims can be found in the work of Anthony Giddens (1984). He argues strongly that it is wrong to understand world history as 'a world growth story'. His view, like that of many other contemporary social scientists, is that 'human history does not have an evolutionary "shape" and positive harm can be done by attempting to compress it into one' (Giddens 1984: 236). His arguments are in line with others discussed earlier.

But while resisting evolutionism of this kind, contemporary social theory at the same time often implicitly, even explicitly, contains hangovers of evolutionary thought. The strong implication remains that of a singular direction, one which cannot be reversed and which will in due course become a feature of all advanced capitalist societies. Giddens himself rejects the notion of 'post-modernity', preferring instead to see a 'late modernity' emerging out of modern society, one which contains elements of continuity (such as the globalization of society) as well as of change (such as the creation of 'manufactured risk') and a 'reflexive modernity' in which people are increasingly making their own biographies. Before either 'modernity' or 'late' (or 'high') modernity there existed, according to Giddens, 'pre-modern' societies, those based on small-scale communities and the establishment of trust based on everyday face-to-face contact.

This is not the place to attempt an understanding of 'post', 'late' or 'high' modernity in these authors or even to discuss the rights and wrongs of their historical account. Of greater concern is the contradiction between their resistance to evolutionism on the one hand and their continued positing of a unilinear sequence (such as pre-modern, modern and late or post-modern) on the other. It would be over-cynical to suggest that social theorists need to periodically announce the arrival of a wholly new kind of modern society in order to justify their existence. The problem is more fundamental than this. Such sequential modes of thinking fail to recognize many of the basic continuities and similarities between these different types of 'modernity'. In particular, these supposedly new social forms all depend on fundamentally similar ways in which class relations, wages systems and surplus product are made and appropriated by a dominant class. These theories also insufficiently recognize the extent to which often similar labour processes in all these societies are using the powers of nature to make and reproduce these supposedly different forms of 'modernity'. But if similarities are not adequately recognized, neither are many of the diversities. Unilinear schemata do not allow, for example, for the possibility that different social forms (and relations to nature) may coexist and indeed be veering off in different 'directions'. These directions are partly a product of the coercive power of global corporations and their capacity for shaping and directing oppositional struggles. But they are also a product of economic relations combining with pre-existing social relations such as those based on race and gender as well as on relationships with local natural resources.

A potentially disastrous legacy from earlier traditions of social and political thought is the continuation and reinforcement of the nature–culture divide. The recent relativist or post-modernist turn is, or possibly was, an important case in point – another example of the drastically over-sociologizing tendency. Particularly relevant to our discussion is work which places great emphasis on the social construction of science. There are many different versions of this tendency, one which at its most extreme refuses to recognize that, while all knowledge is socially constructed, such constructions can refer to an external reality. Perhaps the most obvious example relative to our discussion of social Darwinism is Haraway's (1992) analysis of the ways the 'primate story' has been told. Unlike many social constructionists of the especially 'strong' variety, she does appear to recognize that there is an external world of nature. Nevertheless, the weight of her argument is largely in terms of what she calls 'a triple filter of race, gender and science' (Haraway 1992: 8) 'Biology and primatology', she argues, are

> inherently political discourses, whose chief objects of knowledge, such as organisms and ecosystems, are icons (condensations) of the whole of the history and politics of the culture that constructed them for contemplation and manipulation.
>
> (Haraway 1992: 10)

So while Haraway does not join those relativists who see all knowledge (including scientific knowledge) as no more than a social construction, her inordinate emphasis on the ways in which knowledge is a product of power relations tends to conceal the fact that there may be (indeed is!) some form of reality which social constructions reveal. The danger is essentially that of a slippage between *construction* and *construal*. People can, and indeed have, construed nature how they like. They may well choose, as Haraway and others have pointed out, to equate black people and women with nature and with apes. But such construals need distinguishing from how things are actually constructed.

But such failings are by no means a feature of just the social sciences. The dualism between society and nature has also been rigidly maintained by, for example, many workers in the natural sciences.

On the other hand, writers such as Cavalli-Sforza and Feldman (1981) and Lumsden and Wilson (1981) and a number of others writing in the late 1970s and early 1980s have attempted to see the interaction between cultural and biological evolution (for a review, see Lumsden and Wilson 1981). On the one hand genes and genetic change constrain and enable the production and consumption of ideas. In particular, what Lumsden and Wilson call their 'colonisation' of the mind is seen as closely linked to an individual's reproductive success. Genetic fitness, they believe, is the product of learning and reasoning. One type of social relation, one type of land ownership or exchange system amongst relatives, for example, will be more successful than another in terms of contributing to an individual's reproductive success. Further, culture has had long-term evolutionary consequences 'through an acceleration of neuroanatomical and behavioural evolution unprecedented in the history of life' (Lumsden and Wilson 1981: 7). Unfortunately, however, these authors have given few clues as to the precise mechanisms which were associated with these behavioural changes and forms of human evolution. These should have included discussions of the social relations or modes of production.

Despite the above work, dualistic ways of thought have remained dominant in biological thinking. This becomes particularly clear with, for example, Dawkins's famous book, *The Selfish Gene*, first published in 1976. This is best known for its argument that biological evolution by natural selection operates not at the level of the unit or the species but at the more basic level of the gene. The picture is the popularized and familiar one of organisms being the 'survival machines' of their genes. Given time, copying errors and competition, the design of these machines has, it is argued, improved. Over millions of years, genes, or replicators, have developed increasingly sophisticated 'techniques and artifices' to ensure their continuance in the process of competing to survive. An organism such as a human being is therefore a mere vehicle whose main role is to copy genes and to ensure that they are reproduced into future generations. The gene is the unit which is copied and replicated and, during such processes, small and random errors occur. Such 'errors' affect the success, or otherwise, of the genes' vehicles in coping with their environment.

Much of the debate surrounding *The Selfish Gene* has indeed been concerned with its genetic reductionism. There is a strong element of what Gould (1977) calls 'just-so stories' in Dawkins's account, humans' evolutionary inheritance being used to explain almost any aspect of our behaviour. The same applies to more recent work from 'evolutionary psychology'. This latter field is a rapidly growing and apparently quite popular one (Curry *et al.* 1996). Pinker (1997) is one of the best-known exponents of this area of thought. He describes the mind as

> a neural computer, fitted by natural selection with combinatorial algorithms for causal and probabilistic reasoning about plants, animals, objects and people. It is driven by goal states that served biological fitness in ancestral environments, such as food, sex, safety, parenthood, friendship, status, and knowledge
>
> (Pinker 1997: 524)

Pinker's extension of genetic thinking into psychology again allows almost any kind of behaviour (including selfishness, altruism, sexism, homicide, even our liking for savannah-like landscapes) to our phylogeny, to our evolutionary inheritance and genetically inherited 'hard-wiring'. He tries to avoid the 'just-so story' criticism by the concept of 'reverse engineering'. This entails identifying a goal and specifying the kind of design that would best meet it. How well does the design meet this specification? How well, for example, does the human mind confront the challenges set by both its ancestral and modern environments? But even this modified form of genetic reductionism remains problematic. Not only is it extremely difficult to identify and specify in any detail the problems that human beings confronted on the savannah but it severely underestimates the capacity of humans (and perhaps indeed other animals) to adapt and to coevolve with changing ecosystems and species. This is a matter to which we will return.

Even more problematic, however, has been the attempt to adapt the selfish gene type of analysis back into the sphere of culture. Dawkins (1976: 206) writes:

> I think that a new kind of replicator has recently emerged on this planet. It is still in its infancy, still drifting clumsily about in its primeval soup, but already it is achieving evolutionary change at a rate which leaves the old gene panting far behind.

Dawkins called this new kind of replicator a 'meme'. It is a unit of cultural rather than genetic replication and it obeys the same kinds of rule as the gene, with 'fit' memes, like fit genes, being those that are best at replicating. Examples of memes offered by Dawkins (1996: 206) are 'tunes, catch-phrases, clothes fashions, ways of making pots or building arches'(1976: 206). Meme replicators can be, according to Dawkins, more or less successful. A successful replicator, he argues, has three characteristics. The first is *copying-fidelity*: the more faithful the copy, the more remaining of the initial pattern after several rounds of copying. If, for example, a painting is reproduced by making photocopies from photocopies, the underlying pattern quickly becomes unrecognizable. The second is *fecundity*: the faster the rate of copying, the more the replicator spreads. An industrial printing press can reproduce many more copies of a text than an office copying machine. The third is *longevity*: the longer an instance of the replicating pattern survives, the more copies can be made of it. A drawing made by scratching lines in the sand is, for example, likely to be erased before being reproduced in, for example, the form of a photograph (Heylighen 1996).

Dawkins's work links closely with that of the psychologist Daniel Dennett. For the mind, or the brain, Dennett argues, should be seen as the receiver, transmitter and copier of memes. Memes, he argues,

> now spread around the world at the speed of light, and replicate at rates that make even fruit flies and yeast cells look glacial in comparison. They leap promiscuously from vehicle to vehicle and from medium to medium, and are proving to be virtually unquarantinable.
> (Dennett 1990: 131)

Dawkins and Dennett therefore offer a picture of cultural evolution parallel to biological evolution. As Dawkins (1989: 192) puts it:

> Just as genes propagate themselves in the gene pool by leaping from body to body via sperm or eggs, so memes propagate themselves in the meme pool by leaping from brain to brain via a process which, in the broad sense, can be called imitation.

Runciman (1998) has recently adopted a similar perspective. He, like Dawkins, promotes the 'selectionist paradigm', with the mechanisms of natural selection having, he believes, close similarities with the selection of ideas. He argues that '[i]f the "Darwin-dreaders" are to vindicate their scepticism, they will have to show that the differences which the disanalogies make are such as to undermine the selectionist paradigm as such' (Runciman 1998: 177).

But the problem is not so much 'the selectionist paradigm' but the reductionist, and in the end un-Darwinian, form of the paradigm which it currently takes. With Dawkins and his followers in the cultural sphere we find the problems compounded by yet another analogy between biology and culture, one which further promotes the dualism which has long bedevilled Western thought. Cultural evolution from this perspective is no more than the reproduction of memes 'with errors'. Neo-Darwinists are thereby making the double mistake of not only offering a reductionist form of biology but also offering this same (wrong) model for the understanding of human culture.

Despite all this, so-called 'memetics' is now a fast-developing enterprise. It has a thriving learned society, its own *Journal of Memetics* and an intensely consulted World Wide Web page (http://www.cpm.mmu.ac.uk/jom-emit/). It has also been the subject of a best-selling book (Lynch 1996) and been given considerable coverage in the popular media (Box 5).

Box 5   Viruses of the mind: How odd ideas survive

It all seems perfectly ludicrous: 39 people don their new sneakers, pack their flight bags and poison themselves in the solemn belief that a passing UFO will whisk them off to wonderland. The rest of us have more sense than that, right? Actually, whether we think Jesus died for our sins or assume that the federal government created the AIDS virus, most of us harbour beliefs for which hard evidence is lacking. In fact, our firmest convictions are often the hardest to justify rationally. As one analyst puts it, 'Beliefs that survive aren't necessarily true, rules that survive aren't necessarily fair and rituals that survive aren't necessarily necessary. Things that survive do so because they are good at surviving.'

The new science of memetics takes that observation a step farther. Ideas, according to this model, are a lot like viruses. They thrive as long as they're jumping efficiently from one host to another, and they die out when the chain of transmission is broken. Under the right conditions, even a highly noxious notion can sweep the population like a flu bug. Medical epidemiologists can sometimes predict the scope and course of a disease outbreak just by analysing the structure of a virus. Memetics hasn't achieved such precision, but that is its mission: to explain how beliefs gain currency, and to predict their ebb and flow.

(Excerpt from *Newsweek*, 14 April 1997: 14)

This work is offering simple explanations for very complex processes. Memetics may describe some of the ways in which ideas spread, but it spectacularly fails to investigate why people take up some ideas and not others. Furthermore, memetics does not begin to explain the mechanisms by which ideas become entrenched. An understanding of these complex issues would entail using insights from other disciplines such as social psychology, social theory and politics. Blackmore (1999), one of the most recent exponents of memetics, asks why the tune of a Coca-Cola advertisement goes round her head 'and will not go away'. Her reasoning is that it is a simple meme which is good at reproducing itself, independent of whether such reproduction is of any use to her. This may be part of the explanation, but another part is a multinational corporation ensuring by all means possible that its tunes 'will not go away'. Such are the ways in which Coca-Cola sells over a billion bottles of its drink a day.

Meanwhile, the analogy between biological and cultural evolution again brings severe problems. These include, perhaps most obviously, the unit to which the term 'meme' refers. Lumping together 'tunes, ideas, catch-phrases, clothes fashions' and so on all under the broad category of replicating 'memes' makes the analogy difficult to operationalize. There is the difficult matter of whether or how memes combine with genes. Are they selected for sexual reproducibility? If so, how do we explain unmarried priests, martyrs or kamikaze pilots? Finally, Dawkins briefly suggests that humans have, after all, the special capacity to override the 'tyranny' of their selfish genes with their culture. At this point the theory starts to fall apart. Culture can, after all, override nature. The dualism is still firmly in place.

Finally, the differences between genes and memes are very considerable. For example, genetic theory of the kind developed by Dawkins is based on the assumption that acquired characteristics are not inherited. We also acquire our genes from our parents and no one else. The differences between memes and genes are at least as many as the similarities. Again, the analogy rapidly starts falling apart.

Many of these problems start with the dualism noted: the initial rigid separation between genes and memes. This problem has haunted evolutionary thinking in similar ways well before Dawkins – see, for example, Cavalli-Sforza and Feldman (1981) and Boyd and Richerson (1985). Building a theory based on the interactions between memes and genes seems at first sight like a good way of overcoming this dualism. Perhaps it could be if the units were sensible. But they are not, especially when it comes to 'memes'. This is because memeticists lump ideas of all kinds together into the category of 'memes' and fail to ask how they are made shaped, reproduced, entrenched by the society in which they are 'evolving'. Similarly, Dennett's attempt to link memes and genes by considering the human mind to be meme replicators may look like a successful way of overcoming this dualism but the categories are still highly suspect.

But, even more important, cultural and biological 'evolution' are operating at different levels and are composed of distinct causal mechanisms (Collier 1994; Dickens 1996). Human society is of course subject to biological and evolutionary processes, but it cannot be reduced to these processes or properly understood via such processes. Furthermore, the reproduction of ideas (including the idea that Coca-Cola is an excellent drink) is subject to a very distinctive range of social and economic relations and processes. These processes are under active consideration by cultural sociologists and others and are becoming quite well understood. Analogies with evolution and genes are therefore profoundly and misleadingly unhelpful at this point. Besides, it is by no means clear that genes should anyway be given such prominence even within biology. There are much better ways forward.

The biological and sociological literatures alike, therefore, are still talking past each other. But the problem is by no means all created by natural scientists. Social scientists have largely ignored biology altogether. One rationale for doing this is the argument that biological evolution is now of relatively little significance relative to cultural evolution. Biological evolution can be seen as having largely ceased while human beings have developed the capacity to adapt as a species to almost any circumstance (in particular, the capacity for communication).

Such is, for example, the suggestion of Norbert Elias, a social scientist who, ironically enough, is more sensitive to biological theory than most other social scientists (Elias 1994; Mennell 1989). In *The Civilizing Process* he envisages social change as constituted by the development of small but interdependent units competing for power. 'Some will be victorious and others vanquished' (Elias 1994: 347) The competition, however, becomes increasingly 'refined or sublimated'. In court society in western Europe, for example, monopoly by the powerful was achieved through a civilizing process in which the upper classes steadily learned to control their behaviour, to avoid outward displays of bodily functions and, at the same time, to disapprove of and dominate the lower classes.

According to Elias, then, 'standards' were amongst the increasingly sophisticated ways in which social control was exerted. Again, cultural evolution is seen as displacing biology even if, unlike biological evolution, culture can in some sense 'evolve backwards' from time to time. In *The Civilizing Process* there is a strong sense of direction to the analysis, an implication that it is a process to which all societies will in due course become subject. 'The civilizing process is a change of human conduct and sentiment in a quite specific direction', he suggests (Elias 1994: 445). In his later work, however, he insisted that the emergence of the court society in western Europe was just one form of the civilizing process (Mennell 1989). Presumably he was anxious to resist any suggestion that the particular kind of cultural evolution was the only possible kind.

How does biology fit into Elias's picture? Humans are a remarkably flexible species, he argued. They have the capacity to adapt to many different conditions. They have the potential to learn, communicate, to change their social relations and to domesticate themselves. Furthermore, they have the capacity to resist immediate gratification. Instead of, for example, eating the first thing they find they are able to constrain themselves. Resisting such immediate impulses means, for example, they have been able to think long-term and create technologies to produce food on a large scale and store it until the time it is really needed. In short, they have developed the capacity for abstract thought, and this places them above other animals who are not able to think long-term, remember the past and plan accordingly.

There is much to Elias's argument to take forward into an understanding which links cultural to biological change and overcome the dualisms we have been addressing. On the other hand, there are dangers and difficulties in his approach. First, there remains the danger of avoiding biology altogether – implying, for example, that biological development really no longer matters as a result of human beings' supposed cultural flexibility. Second, human beings' flexibility, capacity for abstract thought and so on need explaining and problematizing. Third, it is not at all clear precisely why these civilizing processes are taking place. There is more than a hint of teleology in Elias: a civilizing 'assumption' is made but without explaining why this process should be occurring. Some of these problems, which are of course by no means unique to Elias, can start to be dealt with if we start to look at ontogeny rather phylogeny.

A way forward: ontogeny and the making of self-identity

Many of the difficulties can be resolved if, in the first instance, we turn to an alternative form of biology, one which concentrates on the organism and its relation to the environment. In this perspective the organism is envisaged as composed of (genetically inherited) powers of growth and development. And rather than just blindly responding to its environment (composed, of course, of other organisms) it is actively involved in making its environment (see, in particular, Lewontin 1982; Rose *et al.* 1984; Dickens 1992; Goodwin 1994). A strong argument could be made that such a perspective is more in line with Darwin's thinking than latter-day 'neo-Darwinism'.

Importantly, however, this perspective does not entail a separation of nature from culture. Humans are indeed a natural sort but – and this is the key point of this chapter – they are a culture-making natural sort as they develop from the earliest stages of their life. At the later stages of this early development process they make their own self-identities in the contexts of their environment. One key way to link the cultural with the natural is therefore via *ontogeny*, the development of the human being from embryo to young adult. Furthermore, this making of identities takes place through humans' active engagement with their social and physical environment.

On the one hand we must recognize the genetically encoded and empirically well-established processes of development which affect all human beings (Woods and Grant 1995; Rose 1997). During the earliest stages of an individual's life the fertilized ovum becomes transformed into two touching hollow balls of cells. Within 18 days there develops a thickening where these two balls meet, this being the *neural groove*. The neural groove develops into the spinal cord and this develops to make the forebrain, midbrain and hindbrain. From this stage onwards the central nervous system develops very rapidly. Cell division takes place, resulting in structures which are very close to their final physical form. By the ninth month of life the essentials of a human being are in place, though further development take places after birth. At six months the brain is 50 per cent of its adult weight, after a year 60 per cent, after six years 90 per cent and after ten years 95 per cent.

If such are the underlying, genetically encoded, developments affecting all human beings, it must also be recognized that the physical structures of the brain (its biochemistry, cellular structure and electrical circuitry) are modified as the human being interacts with the environment. According to Rose (1992), a form of natural selection takes place whereby there is first a massive overproduction of synaptic connections made at the earliest stages of a human's life, but with redundant synapses being discarded in the light of experience. Concepts and recollections are therefore encoded in the brain in terms of complex changes in the neural system, and these come about as the developing human being interacts with her or his environment. Such an approach begins to seriously undermine those who would pose genes as the basis for understanding the relationships between the human organism and environment. Development is not simply encoded by genes. Broad tendencies are genetically inscribed but not determined. This is because the social and physical environment plays a key role in terms of affecting how basic, genetically-based, processes are formed during an individual's development as that individual responds to and indeed changes her or his external environment.

This brings us to a second and central element of this discussion. Human development occurs through work, practical activity or engagement with the outside world. The development of the brain and of consciousness occurs through just such activity. As Piaget and others have pointed out, one of the first reflexes of the developing child is sucking. As Woods and Grant (1995: 300) put it, 'for the new born child, the world is first and foremost something to be sucked'. At the earliest age, a baby tries to 'assimilate' the world to itself, introducing it into its month. As development takes place, however, it begins to 'accommodate' to reality, adjusting to the external environment, slowly distinguishing, perceiving and remembering it. Intelligence develops through engagement with the outside and from practice. Similarly, at about 18 months a child can be expected to develop means to ends, to acquire an object through the use of the stick, for example. Elements of logic, and the relations between cause and effect, start to be established, but again through practical interaction with the outside world.

As discussed in more detail later, the early years of a human's life see the child developing its potential for making and understanding abstract ideas. They also see the development of language. Language is part of an abstraction process which has been particularly well developed by humans. It is a means by which past actions can be reconstructed through interacting with other people and by which future actions and their results can be anticipated. With language humans make themselves *as* humans. They are made able to rise above the constraints of the present, to learn from the past and to plan for the future. And of course language is the means by which culture and tradition are made, passed on and communicated. Language is therefore a means by which humans make both their society and themselves. It is part of the emergence of the distinctly human capacity for abstract thought, though a capacity which is genetically enabled. A view of language or culture along these lines is surely much richer than the somewhat poverty-stricken notion of 'memes'.

This brings us to the third key element of an ontogenetic approach to dealing with the culture–nature schism. The capacity for abstract thinking, albeit abstract thought linked to human activity, not only gives the developing human the capacity to understand distant events and events which have taken or may still take place. It also enables the developing and active child to see itself in relation to the rest of the world, including the rest of the human social world. But this capacity for the development of identity is also genetically inherited. Humans seem to have a particularly well-developed sense of self. This sense of identity emerges during the early development of the child and becomes an integral part of the human's mental structure. Recent research on autism in humans is showing up those parts of the brain necessary for the emergence of this sense of self (Goddard 1998; Frith and Happé 1999). Some elements of self-awareness seem to be a feature of chimpanzees, our nearest relatives. But this potential reaches a much fuller expression with the capacity of humans for creating, making and communicating abstract thought.

The ontogenetic development of the person is therefore a key to the capacity of the human to develop a sense of self. A sense of self-consciousness is a central part of what it is to be human. This is a key way of understanding how the 'cultural' and the 'biological' can be interlinked. It is a point to which we will return.

4

New Forms of
Social Darwinism:
The Bell Curve
and Its Implications

The child of the townsman is bred too fine, it is too great an exagger-
ation of himself, excitable and painfully precocious in its childhood,
neurotic, dyspeptic, pale and undersized in its adult state, if it ever
reaches it . . . If it be not crossed with fresh blood, this town type, in the
third and fourth generations becomes more and more exaggerated . . .
It has been maintained with considerable show of probability that a
pure Londoner of the fourth generation is not capable of existing.
(Dr Freeman-Williams, writing in 1890,
cited in Stedman Jones 1971)

Dr Freeman-Williams was one of a large number of London medical professionals in the late nineteenth century who believed that
the inner London population was suffering from a form of heredi-
tary degeneration. The vast mass of the population at the heart of
the British Empire was going into rapid decline. This was seen as
partly a result of the inner-urban labourer being able to successfully
compete with the innately healthy and sturdy country immigrant.
(The survival of the fittest was still being successfully worked out in
the countryside.) It was also the product of a self-reproducing
underclass in which the inadequacies of one generation were being
passed on to the next. Those excluded, argued the influential econ-
omist Alfred Marshall, 'know nothing of the decencies and the

quiet and very little of the unity of family life and religion fails to reach them' (cited in Macnicol 1987: 297).

Such thinking lay behind the theory of 'urban degeneration', a theory which concentrated wholly on the personal and inherited characteristics of the people themselves, mental and physical inheritances which were clearly inadequate in the Darwinian struggle for survival. This left the middle classes alarmed. Not only was their city in decline but the characteristics of a fast-breeding underclass could only lead to an indefinite increase in the degeneration of the white race.

Is such social Darwinism alive today? The term means many things, but it is particularly well known for suggesting that the success of a human being depends on his or her inborn characteristics. More specifically, it can imply a theory of society in which an underclass is seen as composed of genetically inferior peoples who are in inevitable decline. Furthermore, according to such a view, there is little that can be done about them since, at the time of writing at least, social engineers have not found a way of manipulating the genetic characteristics, and hence the fate, of the underclass.

To many observers and commentators, Dr Freeman-Williams remarks were echoed just over a century later by *The Bell Curve* (Herrnstein and Murray 1994). This book has sold several hundred thousand copies, been the subject of a presidential press conference and of cover stories in many news and opinion magazines. Either because or despite of its impact, it has been subjected to extensive and sometimes vitriolic debate. This chapter will rehearse some of the arguments of this influential book and outline some of the main criticisms which have been mounted against it. On the other hand, some of the participants in these debates have been talking past each other. Herrnstein and Murray place enormous emphasis on the idea of a genetically inherited intelligence. Their critics, by contrast, almost completely reject the possibility of such a genetic inheritance. One way ahead is to accept the significance of genetics for human intelligence and progress but not to attribute massive significance to genes *per se*. The social environment, and how people actively relate to their environment, must also be central to any reasonable account. As we will see, the most recent research on this complex issue is beginning to support such a view. Further, there is a form of biologically-based account which offers a more subtle, if more complex, understanding of this kind.

The emphasis of *The Bell Curve* has often been misunderstood or misrepresented. In particular, it has been argued that its main message concerns the supposed low IQ levels of black people. Its central thesis is about the changing class structure of modern America. It is one based on what Herrnstein and Murray call 'cognitive ability'. It is those who have such an ability, the 'cognitive elite', who are likely to rise into the elite well-paid jobs.

> The twentieth century dawned on a world segregated into social classes defined in terms of money, power, and status. The ancient lines of separation based on hereditary rank were being erased, replaced by a more complicated set of overlapping lines. Social standing still played a major role, if less often accompanied by a sword or tiara, but so did out-and-out wealth, educational credentials and, increasingly, talent. Our thesis is that the twentieth century has continued the transformation, so that the twenty-first will open on a world in which cognitive ability is the decisive dividing force. The shift is more subtle than the previous one but more momentous. Social class remains the vehicle of social life, but intelligence now pulls the train.
>
> (Herrnstein and Murray 1994: 25)

The central idea, then, is that America is a meritocracy. In a society where the premium for successful and well-paid work is intelligence, people are increasingly getting the kinds of jobs for which they are mentally cut out. The intelligentsia of whatever class is being selected (and through interbreeding is selecting itself) to become a cognitive elite – in, for example, the upper echelons of management or education. At the same time, however, and as a reciprocal to the emergence of the cognitive elite, there is said to be an ever-increasing underclass. This is composed of much faster-breeding people with low IQ levels. High IQ is seen by Herrnstein and Murray as becoming the main passport to success. Nothing can be done to raise low levels of IQ. Social or welfare programmes such as Head Start and Affirmative Action are argued to be either useless or even counter-productive. Intervention in its present form is therefore not likely to be productive. Since little can be done to change the inequalities between the cognitive elite and a cognitively weak underclass, the only way forward is 'letting people find valued places in society'.

According to Herrnstein and Murray, IQ is what people generally mean when they use a word like 'intelligent' or 'smart'. But how is it measured? Clearly this is a key part of their argument. First, it should be stressed that there are a number of different versions of factor analysis as applied to IQ. It remains an area of considerable debate (Hunt 1997). Herrnstein and Murray argue that it can be measured accurately by standard intelligence tests. These authors consider themselves to be 'classicists', following on from the work of Spearman. The argument of the classicists is that intelligence can be measured by a single and general measure of intelligence called 'g'. This is defined as a person's capacity for complex mental work and is 'one of the most powerful [measures] for understanding socially significant human variation' (Herrnstein and Murray 1994: 14). Spearman's measure is what they call 'structural' in the sense that it is genetically built into the person being tested. Other measures are considered, though in the end rejected. These latter include those of the 'revisionists'. One of the best-known members of this school of thought is Sternberg (1985). Here the emphasis is on process. The attempt is not that of seeking the elements of intelligence but of establishing what people are actively doing when exercising their intelligence. Sternberg and others within this camp question how much a general measure is really revealing. A person may, for example, be a wonderful visualizer of spatial images but be unable to compose a sentence. A second person may be able to construct the greatest prose but have few spatial abilities. This links to a third approach rejected by Herrnstein and Murray. This is represented by what they call the 'radicals'. This school, of which Howard Gardner is the leading protagonist, rejects any idea of a general 'g'. It argues for a number of distinctive forms of intelligence. These include linguistic, musical, mathematical, spatial and two forms of 'personal intelligence' based on the capacity for forming human relationships.

Herrnstein and Murray stick to the classical definition, arguing that (despite all the controversies) most research workers would agree with six conclusions which derive from classical theory. First, there is indeed, they suggest, such a thing as cognitive ability on which humans differ. Second, all standardized tests of academic aptitude or of achievement are measuring the 'g' factor to some degree, and it is IQ tests which measure this factor most accurately. Third, IQ scores accord with popular parlance. They do place a measure on what people mean they use words like 'intelligent' or 'smart'. Fourth, IQ scores are to a large degree stable (though, they admit, not totally stable) over an individual's lifetime. Fifth, if properly administered,

IQ tests are not biased against class, ethnic or racial groups. Finally, they suggest that cognitive ability is to a large degree heritable. According to Herrnstein and Murray this is not less than 40 per cent and no more than 80 per cent. In short, Herrnstein and Murray are saying that while there may be problems with a general measure of IQ, it is a fairly simple and rough-and-ready measure which in some sense 'works' and which allows research to be carried out on significant social trends such as the development of a new class structure based on cognitive ability.

Using the National Longitudinal Survey of Youth which started in 1979 (in which a group of approximately 13,000 young people aged 12–21 are interviewed annually) the authors show that the cognitive ability measured by IQ tests reliably predicts (albeit with sometimes weak levels of correlation) people's professional, academic and pecuniary success. As mentioned earlier, *The Bell Curve* is perhaps best known, probably unjustly, for its suggestion that IQ levels are distributed unevenly between races and ethnic groups. It suggests African-Americans have an IQ about 15 points below that of Caucasians, with the IQ of the latter being in turn lower (by about 5 points) than that of East Asians. The book also suggests, rather in the same way as the nineteenth-century urban degenerationists with whom we started this chapter, that these inequalities are augmented as a result of people usually marrying others with similar IQs. The poor transmit their low IQs and consequently their poverty. Their higher rates of fecundity are threatening a decline in the general population's genetic potential for IQ. Furthermore, single mothers with low IQs are less likely to provide the kinds of social environment that will help their children. *The Bell Curve*, incidentally, is much less adventurous when it comes to consider gender as distinct from ethnic differences. It argues very briefly that men and women have on average nearly identical IQs, but that men have more representation at either end of *The Bell Curve*. The bell shape is therefore flatter for men, there being more smart and more dull men despite the mean being virtually the same for the genders.

The combination of high fertility rates and welfare inputs means, then, that a society such as the United States must confront the likelihood of a self-inflating, cognitively deficient and criminally inclined underclass, one which will pose no end of problems to the continued progress of the most powerful nation on earth. The sexual revolution, the declining support to the family by the state and the fact that 'it has become much more difficult for a person of low cognitive ability to figure out why marriage is such a good thing' (Herrnstein and Murray 1994: 544) all lead to the continuing expansion of the underclass. The process, according to Hernnstein and Murray, has spatial implications. The outmigration of the ablest black people 'has left the inner city without its former leaders and role models, (Herrnstein and Murray 1994: 522). Again, the recommendation is that of recognizing that little can be done by governments. People must find the slots for which they are genetically best fitted and they must be encouraged to feel valued, despite taking up positions which may not be well rewarded from a financial viewpoint. This links back to earlier arguments by Murray (1988) that for happiness and self-esteem to be true happiness and self-esteem they must be self-generated.

One counter-argument is that Herrnstein and Murray are strong on ideology and weak on offering understanding. This is because they are content with correlations and do not probe the mechanisms and processes underlying these correlations. So in the end the fact that people with low IQs get either poorly rewarded jobs or no jobs at all is explained by their IQ levels. This means that other factors, such as the many kinds of discrimination in the workplace, are not treated as part of the analysis. Sowell (1995: 77) is one author who makes such a point.

> Perhaps the most troubling aspect of *The Bell Curve* from an intellectual standpoint is its authors' uncritical approach to statistical correlations. One of the first things taught in introductory statistics is that correlation is not causation.

A second view is that Herrnstein and Murray strongly imply that genetics is fixed and is destiny. This again links to the insistence that other processes and relations may be important in allocating people to jobs and social positions. If it can be proved that certain people are somehow 'naturally' left at the bottom of the social heap and that social welfare provision is likely to be unproductive, then this denies any responsibility for American society to do anything material to improve the conditions of people with low IQs and for blacks. The analysis lets American society, and by implication many other societies, off the hook.

A third set of arguments suggests that the book is out-and-out racism. Although only a small proportion of the book is concerned with ethnic and racial differences in cognitive ability, this is clearly the issue which raises most hackles. There are many counter-arguments. It stands accused of selectively using evidence which supports its politics (Rosen and Lane 1995), wilfully misinterpreting countervailing evidence (Nisbett 1995; Ramos 1995), creating supposedly respectable findings which it actually knows will find favour in the current economic and political climate (Lind 1995), re-exhuming old forms of social Darwinism (Gould 1995) and creating proto-Nazi solutions to supposedly inferior races (Judis 1995).

A final argument, though one which is surprisingly rare, concerns Herrnstein and Murray's central thesis (Wolfe 1995). In what sense is knowledge at a premium in American and other Western societies? How adequate are these authors' understanding of the rise and rise of a 'cognitive elite'? Herrnstein and Murray treat these developments as acts of God when, as discussed later, they are a major site of social struggle. Elites maintain their position precisely through creating a sphere of knowledge separate from understandings based on practical, everyday life. Elites have long made themselves *as* elites in just this way. Furthermore, the authors of *The Bell Curve* seem unaware of (increasingly polarized) social relations in the USA and elsewhere. The comfort of the affluent 'cognitive elites' crucially depends on the work of low-paid and ill-educated classes of people.

It is clear that there are some extremely contentious issues here, and they deserve careful dissection. Notable, however, are the ways in which *The Bell Curve* has been made a political football. On the one hand, it is clear that it has been leapt on and probably supported by powerful conservative forces. Critics of *The Bell Curve* point to its funding by the Bradley Foundation, a politically conservative organization with assets of $240 million. Their support of Herrnstein and Murray's study forms, it is argued, part of a wider attempt to create a set of far-right think tanks and media outlets. The aim, according to one view, is to create an 'alternative academia'.

Meanwhile, antagonism towards *The Bell Curve* has been largely led by left-liberal academics and media sources. They tend to ascribe any blame for inequalities and social differences to society and not to genetically inherited capacities or incapacities. They therefore go to the other extreme in denying that genetics has any influence at all on social stratification and social change. 'Not in

Our Genes', as an early attack on biologically-based accounts of intelligence was entitled (Rose *et al*. 1984).

There are dangers in all this, not least for the political left. Why should biologically-based accounts be the sole province of the right while the left backs itself into the impossible corner of suggesting that biology does not matter? Perhaps even more seriously, are we to assume that science consists solely of the competing arguments between social scientists (and some scientists) with political axes to bear? Hacker, one of the few more balanced commentators on *The Bell Curve*, recognizes that the book has a number of faults. Perhaps its main contribution is to shake the confidence which the different sciences have in their own understandings.

> Richard Herrnstein and Charles Murray have written a book that deserves reflection and respect. The hallmark of a serious study is not simply that it raises its readers to argue, but that it compels them to review their own assumptions.
>
> (Hacker 1995: 97)

Intelligence: 'knowns and unknowns'

The debate now shows signs of moving on beyond simplistic power-play between people and disciplines who are talking past each other. An arguably more dispassionate view of these complex matters is a review of the intelligence debate by the Board of Scientific Affairs of the American Psychological Association (APA) – Neisser *et al*. (1996). This is a rapidly developing field, however. There remain many uncertainties, and it is almost certainly impossible to exclude politics and ideology from this matter.

The APA report at least recognizes that there can be many different forms of intelligence. Some people may, for example, thrive when it comes to tests of verbal ability and others may do well on spatial aptitudes. (They may, for example, have no difficulty when it comes to drawing the opposite to a shape with which they are confronted.) Nevertheless, there are significant correlations between different types of intelligence. As the authors put it, 'subtests measuring different abilities tend to be positively correlated: people who score high on one such subtest are likely to be above average on others as well' (Neisser *et al*. 1996: 78). This was also the finding of Spearman (1927), who was first responsible for 'g', his measure of a general capacity for complex mental work. There remains difficulty in defining what exactly 'g' is, but it nevertheless seems a reasonable first shot at assessing general intellectual capacity.

But it is also clear that in many ways the picture is far less clear than that advanced by *The Bell Curve*. First, one of the more interesting parts of their report concerns the stability, or otherwise, of test scores. It argues that intelligence tests scores are fairly stable during development. But the report admits that it is difficult to measure the intelligence of young children. Child psychology such as that from Piaget suggests that human beings gain rapidly-increasing capacities during their early years, especially in terms of verbal expertise and reasoning. But this is very difficult to assess with IQ tests. Furthermore, conventional intelligence tests on infants provide a poor predictor of later test scores, even if they offer good early indications of attention spans and memory. Intelligence test scores remain 'fairly stable' during early years, however, in the sense that scores remain much the same between individuals of the same age. Nevertheless, there can be important change over time. One study cited by Neisser *et al.* showed that the average change between ages 12 and 17 was 7.1 points, with some individuals' IQs changing by as much as 18 points.

Second, the report examined the relationship between IQ and the acquisition of good education and jobs. School achievement is highest amongst those with the highest IQ levels, the implication being that children who are more receptive to education are more likely to be encouraged by teachers. Perhaps unsurprisingly, the report finds that the acquisition of social status and income is related not just to IQ but to the social status and income of the parents (though there is a high degree of overlap between the two). Perhaps more surprising, though less so with the benefit of hindsight, is the suggestion that IQ scores may not be the be-all and end-all of success in employment. As we have seen, one of the critiques of Herrnstein and Murray is that they present little evidence of the 'cognitive elite' being sucked out of all classes into the best jobs. Employers are not necessarily looking just for high IQ levels. Interpersonal skills and aspects of personality may be just as important. Such qualities turn out, according to the APA, to be useful additional predictors of success. Furthermore, jobs themselves are not just slots into which premoulded people are fitted. As the APA report points out, a job may help people to realize their so far unrealized capacities. One

study cited by Neisser *et al.* (Kohn and Schooler 1973) suggested that
jobs entailing high levels of flexibility actually had the effect of train-
ing people up to produce greater 'intellectual flexibility'.

This brings us to the important question of environment – physical and biological as well as social. There are, for example, close
links between the biological environment and physical development. Malnutrition, exposure to toxic substances, prenatal and
perinatal stress factors can all result in lower measured intelligence
levels. But the social and cultural environment can also be expected
to have major effects on an individual's skills and IQ levels. Intelligence cannot be simply put down to genes. An example given by
Neisser *et al.* (1996: 86–7) makes the point well:

> Rice farmers in Liberia are good at estimating quantities of rice;
> children in Botswana, accustomed to story-telling, have excellent
> memories for stories. Both these groups were far ahead of American
> controls on the tasks in question. On the other hand Americans and
> other Westernized groups typically out-perform members of tra-
> ditional societies on psychometric tests, even those designed to be
> 'culture-fair.'

In short, levels of IQ cannot be simply ascribed to genes. This is
central to the argument about supposed differences in intelligence
between blacks and whites and between men and women. Neiser *et
al.* recognize the different IQ levels achieved by blacks and whites.
But they argue that there is no evidence to suggest that these different levels of intelligence can be ascribed to genetics. One of the
main problems here concerns the diversity of so-called 'races'.
Observable physical characteristics such as skin colour suggest a
homogeneity which, in genetic terms, is simply not present (for a
discussion see Box 6). In the end, the report plumps for a combination of 'environmental' causes (in particular, low-paid jobs, poor
nutrition, poor schooling and so forth) and continuing differences
between the cultural priorities and practices of African-American
culture and that of the dominant white society.

As regards sex differences, Neisser *et al.* suggest that most IQ
measurements are designed so that there are no overall score
differences between males and females. On the other hand, recent
studies do show some important differences. Males, for example,
seem better at visual-spatial tasks, while females are favoured when
it comes to verbal fluency. Unlike the differences between so-called
'races', however, it seems likely that there are biological as well as

---

Box 6   Social Darwinism and 'race'

What is a 'race'? Darwin himself was convinced that all human races share a common ancestry and belong to the same species. And yet he reflected the values of his time in seeing 'lower' races as having less intelligence and (because they had smaller heads than whites) being less intelligent. These were the factors leading, he believed, to their eventual decline towards extinction when competing with white colonists (Bowler 1990).

Contemporary views of 'race' reject such thinking. They point to the fact that there is as much (if not more) genetic variation between 'races' as there is between local populations. 'Asian-Americans', for example, may have roots in Korea, Laos, Vietnam, the Philippines, India and Pakistan, as well as in China and Japan. It is now very rare to acknowledge race as a biological or theoretically useful category. Indeed, it is more usually seen as a discourse enabling powerful groups to categorize the 'other', to exploit the 'other' and to define themselves as dominant (see, for example, Bond and Gilliam 1994).

A recent view returns to Darwin's original insistence on common ancestry. There may have been an original biological reality to race, but the priority now is to track the growing complexity of races as they split into separate breeding populations over time. Andreasen (1998) uses the concept of 'clades' to describe breeding subspecies which once had a common origin. Such 'cladistic' categorizations are, however, a long way from most popular concepts of 'race'. The folk category 'Asian' is not a cladistic race.

---

social processes involved. On the one hand young girls are still socialized at an early age to behave in certain ways. On the other hand they argue that there are real differences in the neural structures of males and females and that these differences may be in part due to hormonal influences.

Particularly in turning to the social environment, there may be complex reciprocal relationships involved. Children with high IQ levels, for example, may be especially drawn to education at school or higher levels. Certain kinds of jobs may attract certain people with certain kinds of skill. (A teaching job, for example, might attract people, perhaps women in particular, with high levels of verbal dexterity.) The relationships between schools and children may also be far more complex than Herrnstein and Murray suggest.

The APA study suggests, for example, that state interventions intended to upgrade levels of intelligence may be more effective than is sometimes thought. 'Head Start' programmes do seem to raise IQ levels, at least during the course of the teaching process. And in line with Herrnstein and Murray, these gains decline over time and by the end of schooling there are no significant gains in IQ levels. On the other hand, follow-up studies show that children allocated to such programmes are less likely to be allocated to special education later and more likely to finish school later (Sylva 1997). It would therefore be difficult to justify withdrawing such programmes simply on the grounds that children with high IQs will always win through while those with low levels will fail.

There are two remaining features of the summary offered by Neisser *et al.* They are extraordinarily significant and should form a central part of any new kind of 'social Darwinism'. One of these is the so-called 'Flynn effect'. This refers to the steady and well-documented world-wide rise in intelligence test performance. The average is about three IQ points per decade. Work in the Netherlands suggests that the rate of gain may even be increasing. Why is the Flynn effect taking place? This is a matter of considerable debate and the reasons are still by no means clear.

First there is the continuing question of definitions. Flynn himself believed that IQ measurements are suspect and that what we are witnessing is a rise of 'abstract problem solving ability'. (We should remember here, however, the argument that IQ levels can be used as a simple measure of a range of different capacities.) A second possibility is the increasing benefits of better nutrition. Perhaps, therefore, in addition to increasing our physical characteristics (such as height) through better diets we are also improving our intellectual capacities. A third possibility is the changing context within which people are developing. Compared to our forebears, we are engaging in many more various forms of social and cultural engagement with the social world. As Neisser *et al.* (1996: 90) put it: 'These changes in the complexity of life may have produced corresponding changes in the complexity of mind, and hence in certain psychometric abilities.'

The two latter explanations again emphasize the importance of reciprocal relations between the genome (the genetically constituted individual) and its environment. Human beings are engaging with the biological and social environment and manipulating it. At the same time, such manipulation itself may itself be contributing to a form of self-evolution. Humans, knowingly or otherwise, may therefore be participating in their own development. Work by scientists such as Robert Plomin (who has actively supported the work of Herrnstein and Murray) is argued by some to run the risk of not adequately recognizing this complexity. Newspaper articles suggested that he had found the first gene to influence IQ levels (Box 7).

Box 7   Scientists discover gene that creates human intelligence

By Roger Highfield, Science Editor

The first gene that influences human intelligence has been found by scientists, a discovery with huge social and educational implications. The research could herald the development of genetic tests to target potential high-flyers, pave the way to IQ-boosting drugs and will raise fears that embryos that lack smart genes could be aborted. The gene, believed to be the first of many that contribute to normal intelligence, has been found after a six-year search by a team headed by Prof. Robert Plomin of the Institute of Psychiatry in London . . . 'I really think this is a breakthrough', he said. Neuroscientists will now study how this gene works to affect the functioning of the brain, ending years of argument over whether genes can affect intelligence. 'It is harder to argue with a piece of DNA,' he said. . . .

The find marks the first piece of the puzzle of how genetics contributes to human intellect, compared with influences such as education and upbringing. 'It is going to change the way we think about human beings,' said Jonathan Glover, a philosopher at Oxford University. He said many people had not wanted to believe there was a genetic component.

'It has huge social and educational implications,' he said. 'Should we invest in people who have more potential, or should we compensate those who have possibly less genetic potential?' However, Dr David Kind, editor of *GenEthics News*, who has campaigned against Prof. Plomin's research, said the discovery would harden the public belief in genetic determinism, that everything we are is determined by genes. As a Jew, he was 'horrified' by the eugenic implications, for instance, in the screening of unborn children.

(*Daily Telegraph*, 31 October 1997)

On closer inspection, however, the scientific claims made by Plomin and his colleagues are much more modest (Plomin *et al.* 1994; Chorney *et al.* 1998). They do indeed claim to have found a gene (*IGF2R*) associated with a high 'g' level of intelligence. But, as they admit, this only accounts for a small proportion of genetic influences on 'g'. Furthermore, most individuals with high 'g' levels do not even have the particular form of the gene (the 'allele') associated with high 'g' levels. 'It is doubtful', Plomin *et al.* (1994: 116) argue, 'whether enough allele associations will ever be identified that, in combination, can reach levels of prediction that rival those that can be made at present on the basis of parental IQ'.

This again raises the whole question of environment. Research which focuses on, for example, the 'maternal environment' suggests that work such as that by Plomin and Hernnstein and Murray greatly exaggerates the importance of heritability of IQ. The latter authors' estimate was that heritability accounts for 60 per cent of IQ. Daniels *et al.* point to the fact that much of the brain's growth takes place at the earliest stages of the child's life, including life *in utero*, and they produce statistics on twins' development to argue that factors such as the mother's diet, alcohol consumption, drug use and cigarette consumption have a particular significance, one which considerably reduces the relative significance of genes (for further discussion, see McGue 1997; Robertson 1999).

Before we progress to further work in this complex and controversial area, we should note that one of the most fascinating things about the research reported in Neisser *et al.*, and which we also pick up later in this study, is that the effects of genes on IQ become more important as an individual gets older:

> Genes contribute substantially to individual differences in intelligence test performance, and . . . their role seems to increase from infancy to adulthood . . . Variations in the unique environments of individuals are important, and . . . between-family variation contributes significantly to observed differences in IQ scores in childhood although this effect diminishes later on.
>
> (Neisser *et al.* 1996: 86)

Psychologists from Freud and Piaget onwards point to early childhood as having key formative effects (including, in Freud's case, of course, effects on mental well-being) on our later life. This work on the relations between genetics and IQ points to some of the biological mechanisms underpinning such theories.

Social mobility and individual characteristics: more recent research

Another recent argument concerning the importance of biologically inherited differences (though not an argument which attempts to link race to intelligence) is made by Saunders (1996, 1997). This concerns the factors affecting social mobility in contemporary Britain. Using as his empirical basis the results of Britain's large-scale National Child Development Survey, he argues that individual ability and individual effort together play a very large part in social ability, that is, in the social class in which an individual finishes up. On this basis individuals tend to finish up with the job for which they are best fitted and for which they have (or have not) worked. Accountants and lawyers have very high IQ levels (IQ being a measure of a connected set of potentials such as verbal reasoning and spatial abilities) whereas miners and farmhands are at the lowest end of the IQ scale. Success, therefore, tends to await those who are genetically better endowed with intelligence and those who, through exercising effort, work on realizing these capacities. Correspondingly, the social advantages and disadvantages surrounding an individual therefore have much less importance than is conventionally supposed. As Saunders (1996: 72) concludes:

> If we are interested in identifying those factors which play the most important role in determining the social class positions which we all end up in, then we should be paying far more attention to factors to do with individuals themselves – especially their ability and their motivation – and we should be worrying much less than we have done about the effects of the social situations into which they are born and within which they grow up.

Furthermore, the situation is believed by Saunders to be self-exacerbating in the sense that the middle classes with high IQs tend to mate with other middle-class people with high IQs, while working-class parents tend to produce children with lower IQs than middle-class couples. However, the implication in both Saunders's work and in *The Bell Curve* is not, as might be expected, a growing concentration of affluent and intelligent people on the one hand and poor people of low intelligence on the other. This is because of what these writers call 'regression to the mean'. Some children of 'bright' parents are less 'bright', some children of 'average' parents are 'bright' and so on.

Saunders's work has generated a good deal of debate. This has focused on what some see as his overemphasis on inbuilt or genetically inherited capacities and his underemphasis of class, education, housing conditions and so forth in terms of denying or improving life chances. They also concentrate on whether and how it is possible to actually measure 'effort' (Breen and Goldthorpe 1998; Marshall and Swift 1996; Savage and Egerton 1997). *The Bell Curve* has generated even more debate. Again, what is 'IQ' actually measuring? Can such a measure sum up the range of human capacities (thinking, symbolizing and interacting with the environment) of which humans are capable? Patterson (1995: 196) takes this point to its fullest extreme:

> Whatever it is that IQ tests are measuring, whatever it is that *g* is, – whether it be some Platonic ideal, or *g* for ghost, a pun which Ryle might not have intended when he dismissed the whole thing in his Concept of Mind as 'the ghost in the machine' – it could have nothing to do with those vitally important behavioural qualities that meaningfully account for our survival in both broad evolutionary and narrower sociological terms.

Yet these arguments and dismissals again run the risk of ignoring the crucial *relationships* between biology and society. The danger is that of reproducing the old dualism between biology and society. Furthermore, biological explanations are espoused by the right and social explanations by the left. How can this arid dichotomization be overcome? It is via a recognition that biologically evolved capacities in human beings can be either promoted or denied by social systems and social institutions.

Ways forward

Insisting on seeing organisms, including human beings, in their context leads almost inevitably to a more complex and uncertain picture. But, as outlined in more detail later, modern developmental and evolutionary biology is now providing some important clues as to the value of such an approach.

On the one hand it is clear that influences on a young and growing child are indeed likely to be very important (Devlin *et al.* 1997). We noted earlier, for example, that a baby's brain is not fully formed at birth. Its physiological, neurological and cognitive development occurs during the earliest months and years of its life and its environment is indeed particularly important at these earliest stages.

On the other hand, while such impairment may not be easy to change, neither has it become genetically coded or permanently fixed. This fixing seems to happen a good deal later in the life of humans, and indeed of other species. How development relates to evolution by natural selection is a core theme in contemporary biological thought. At one time the theory of 'recapitulation' held sway, in which it was supposed that the development of an organism was a repeat of its evolutionary history. Now that theory has been abandoned, not least because it is realized that at the earliest stages of their development related animals demonstrate more differences than they do at the later stages of their lives. At the same time, it is now recognized that development and evolution are indeed connected in complex ways. As Maynard Smith (1998: 3) puts it: 'Development depends on genetic information that has been accumulated over millions of years of evolution, and the evolution of adult forms has depended on developmental changes in successive generations.'

So development is not driven by evolution but it depends on genetic information acquired during the evolutionary process. Evolution, on the other hand, depends on genetic information and on developmental changes in successive generations. Again, the precise relationships between these two processes are still not clear. However, it now seems very unlikely that genetic change to organisms does not take place at the so-called 'phylotopic' stage of development, the earliest stage at which the basic differentiated features of the organism are present in their final positions. Genetic change at this stage would almost certainly be too drastic. Evolution by natural selection takes place through very small changes, and such modifications at the phylotopic stage would entail too great and sudden a change. The relationship between development and evolution by natural selection is more likely, it seems, to take place through evolution taking up genetic change at *later* stages in the organism's life. Later on, the different parts of the organism become relatively autonomous and divided into relatively separate modules. Growth and development of these modules can take place by natural selection, without wholesale change to the organism and without large-scale risk to future generations (Maynard Smith 1998).

As will be clear, it is much too early to be entirely confident about the relationships between human development and evolution. The most important lesson to come from this review is to consider the developing human organism in context. The question arises, however, as to precisely how this relation should be specified. Perhaps the most satisfactory way forward is to consider the human organism (and any kind of organism) as consisting of a set of potentials, capacities and developmental tendencies. These are genetically inherited. But how, indeed whether, these work out in practice depends on the social and physical environment. In these ways the dichotomies organism–environment, nature–culture, genes–environment become disposed of. Both strictly relate to the other.

5

An Evolved
Human Nature?

Social Darwinism in its many forms contains a number of assumptions about human nature. What is our own nature, what Marx called our 'species-being'? How does this nature relate to our kind of society? Are we an essentially competitive or solidaristic type of animal? There has been much speculation over these questions, and they remain an area of continuing uncertainty and debate. Recent work in ethology and evolutionary psychology has led to renewed speculation. This chapter suggests that arguments around human nature have often been over-simplistic. It moves towards a new way of linking Darwinism and social thought.

There are two obvious starting-points here. The first suggests that humans are essentially individualistic killer-apes with innate propensities towards aggression, blood-lust and violence. This is the picture painted by, amongst others, Ardrey (1961) and Chagnon (1992). The argument is that we have inherited these tendencies as a result of our long history as hunter-gatherers. It is a picture developed more recently as an attempt to understand male violence. Thus Wrangham and Peterson (1977: 173) appeal to Darwinian theory as follows: 'Better fighters tend to have more babies. That's the simple, stupid, selfish logic of sexual selection'. According to this perspective, therefore, capitalism, war, slavery, colonialism and sexism are a direct product of our evolutionary inheritance. The other view is that humans are inherently mutualistic, cooperative and collectively-minded.

Therefore, the argument goes, the individualistic and hierarchical society in which we live runs directly counter to our evolved human nature. There are many authors who could be taken as representing these alternative positions. This chapter takes Maryanski and Turner as broadly reflecting the first point of view, and the anarchist writers Kropotkin and Bookchin as representing the second. The matters covered in this chapter are highly complex and controversial. It will be concluded, however, that neither of these positions is correct. On the one hand humans, and no doubt other species, are composed of no single set of behavioural predispositions. They have inherited a number of alternative potentials as regards their behaviour and it is difficult to predict in advance which one of these will be predominant. It is easier to talk of certain constraints and potentials associated with human beings. These include the need to eat, seek shelter and reproduce. These are needs which can of course be realized in a number of ways, and indeed may not be realized at all. Furthermore, humans have the distinctive power to conceptualize, to communicate and to link abstract concepts with experientially-based knowledge. These are a feature of what Marx called their 'species-life'. They are the product of the evolutionary process through which they have passed as we have coevolved with other species and attempted to survive and reproduce.

There are a number of opportunities here for distinct political positions. To a large extent the argument that humans are instinctively competitive and individualistic comes from liberal and conservative thinkers, while the argument that we are essentially mutualistic (with modern society having wrecked this mutualism) comes from socialist and anarchist thought. This chapter will argue, however, that neither political perspective can take comfort in the notion of an essential human nature. The picture is more complex than that, the dichotomy between 'competitive individualism' and 'mutualism' being over-drawn.

Maryanski and Turner can be used as contemporary representations of the view that human beings have inherited essentially competitive and individualistic instincts. (Maryanski and Turner 1992; Maryanski 1992). Their argument can be summarized around two key points. They suggest that human beings are essentially individualistic, drawing their conclusion from an examination of the nature of social relations amongst present-day Old World monkeys and apes. From this study they deduce the social structure of what they call 'the last common ancestor' and, hence, the nature of humans' own nature. Monkeys have a high density of network ties and apes a low density of such ties. The last common hominoid ancestor is reconstructed as composed of 'a loosely organised horde, with the mother/child tie being the only stable grouping' (Maryanski 1992: 21). Low levels of sociality and high levels of individualism were therefore the essential feature of our distant ancestors and these characteristics still predominate in contemporary human beings.

Interestingly, Maryanski and Turner interpret hunter-gatherer societies as demonstrating their point about the individualism of human nature. They stress, as have many other authors, the relative lack of imposed authority of formal legal codes or formal education. Societies of hunters and gatherers, they argue, 'come close to being a fully egalitarian system' (Maryanski and Turner 1992: 85) with such few social distinctions as exist being based on age and gender rather than ownership of resources. Maryanski and Turner briefly refer, as again have others, to those norms and values in many hunting and gathering societies which place a special premium on sharing and cooperation. On the other hand, these authors choose to emphasize that such societies placed, and continue to place 'a strong emphasis on "individualism" and "self-reliance"' (Maryanski and Turner 1992: 84).

Despite their arguments regarding genetically-based individualism, however, Maryanski and Turner are not saying that humans are asocial. Rather, they argue that such sociality was imposed on us by modern culture. This brings us to the second element of Maryanski and Turner's argument. If human beings are essentially individualistic there is in modern societies, they suggest, a severe clash between this predisposition and the social relations which as a human species we have formed. Marriage, domestic relations, kinship units, monarchies, companies and state bureaucracies are all part of the 'social cage' to which Maryanski and Turner's book title alludes. The tensions, aggressions and territorial competitions of which we are well aware are all products of this clash. They are not in themselves a product of any aggressive or territorial instincts. Rather, they are a result of our human nature being suppressed by modern institutions. But this is not to say that the future is bleak. According to Maryanski and Turner, modern society is still emancipatory. This is because citizenship, democracy and the market all allow human beings' individualism to be recognized. Citizenship and democracy keep imposed authority at bay while markets allow people to realize their innate yet neglected needs for choice and the expression of individuality. Thus they feel able to conclude that 'for all the early sociologists' deep concern with "the loss of community," in truth ordinary people embrace the chance to live and participate in a system relatively well attuned to their primate heritage' (Maryanski and Turner 1992: 162).

In these ways, therefore, Maryanski and Turner attempt to turn much of social theory on its head. 'Anomie', 'alienation' and 'estrangement' are common features of the classical sociological literature. The explicit or implicit message is that humans as a species are out of step with the very society they have made. It is a version of a similar message in later social theory. Freud (1987), for example, is especially well known for arguing that our biology is repressed by the demands of contemporary civilization. A similar picture comes from Elias, discussed earlier. But if Maryanski and Turner are right, there is no fundamental problem with the relation between contemporary society and human nature. Humans are now to a large degree realizing their inborn propensity towards individualism and the lack of close-knit community.

However, this conclusion, like others from an opposing political perspective, contains a strong element of assertion and wishful thinking. A picture of an *essentially* cooperative humanity is offered by contemporary anarchists. Kropotkin, for example, argued strongly that 'mutual aid' was a fundamental part of human beings' biological make-up (Kropotkin 1987). He claimed to show that cooperation, rather than competition, was a fundamental part of all animals' make-up and that this could be observed throughout human history. And what applied to nature as a whole applied to human nature:

> Those species which best know how to combine, and to avoid competition, have the best chances of survival and of further progressive development. They prosper, while the unsociable species decay. It is evident that it would be quite contrary to all that we know of nature if men were an exception to so general a rule.
>
> (Kropotkin 1987: 74)

Competition was therefore seen by Kropotkin as the exception rather than the rule. Collaboration and care, he argued, are more central to survival than competition, stemming largely from the necessary care of progeny. Such collective behaviour, Kropotkin argued, was a central feature amongst 'savages' – during, that is, the period when we emerged as human beings.

A similar picture, though one which places rather less emphasis on the notion of an evolved human nature, comes from the contemporary anarchist Murray Bookchin (1982, 1989). He argues strongly that collaboration is an inherent feature of the human societies, one which has its source in parental relationships (Bookchin 1989: 27). However, to a lesser extent than Kropotkin, he is concerned to explore the dialectical relations between society *and* nature, including human nature. His account of gender divisions, for example, argues that what started out as a biological tie based on feeding between mother and child became institutionalized into male-dominated hierarchies in early hunting societies. As bands of hunter-gatherer societies increased in size and number, men acquired for themselves increasing mobility and prowess to defend their communities. These spontaneously constructed divisions of labour were the beginnings, what Bookchin calls the 'natural' beginnings, of more permanent forms of domination which separated domestic life from civil society. And, as part of this process, domestic life, woman's nurturing capacities, her supposed 'feminine characteristics' became subordinated while men's innate capacities also become distorted and misused and institutionalized.

> The woman's nurturing capacities are degraded to renunciation; her tenderness to obedience. Man's 'masculine' traits are also transformed. His courage turns into aggressiveness; his strength is used to dominate; his self-assertiveness is transformed into egotism; his decisiveness into repressive reason. His athleticism is directed increasingly to the arts of war and plunder.
>
> (Bookchin 1982: 80)

Bookchin's approach therefore is quite cautious about any notion of inbuilt essences or propensities derived from our evolution. Nevertheless, he argues that hierarchical and dominating social relationships are uniquely associated with human society and cannot be found in non-human societies. To that extent humans are out of step with the rest of nature, having institutionalized domineering relations towards women, children and nature as a whole. In so far as humans are envisaged by Bookchin as a product of evolution, they are what he calls 'second nature' (Biehl 1997). Human beings are the self-conscious part of nature, clearly a result of evolution but a species that plans ahead and actively shapes its own development.

Bookchin's analysis also extends well beyond human nature to include relations with external nature. He sees the slow development of a male-orientated culture as closely related to the rise of a separation of people from nature and a domineering temperament towards not only people but also the non-human world. The institutionalized power of one group of people over another is directly associated with environmental degradation. The exploitation of people has gone hand in hand with the exploitation of nature.

One key point to note here about Bookchin's work is his great emphasis on the category 'mutualism' and his parallel rejection of predation and 'individualism'. And yet, as Rudy (1998: 83) has pointed out, 'mutualism' and his linked assertion of 'symbiotic' relations between species are very complex categories, can cover a wide range of practices:

> Bookchin fails to address the diverse and differentiated forms of ecological relations associated with the terms 'mutualism' and 'symbiosis.' Mutualism, the beneficial interaction between species, and symbiosis, the close association of interspecies life patterns, remain incompletely understood as a result. For example, mutualistic relations range from those which are characterised by direct beneficial interaction to those which are indirectly beneficial; direct mutualistic relations can be symbiotic, closely and immediately associated, or non-symbiotic, distantly and contingently associated.

More importantly still, Bookchin remains blinkered to the vast range of relationships which exist in nature. These include mutualism, but they also include commensalism (different species sharing the same resources), predatory relationships as well as outright competition. This critique of Bookchin therefore alerts us to the distinct possibility that the dichotomy 'individualism versus mutualism' is far too over-drawn.

An evolved human nature? Recent research

Many of these debates about the nature of human nature are lacking in terms of empirical evidence. Yet recent work in anthropology, social psychology and medical sociology appears to show that the picture drawn by these authors is wrong – or at the very least it suggests that there remains considerable room for debate. Any such debate would start by appraising the period during which human beings evolved from their pre-human ancestors. This is the era during which they developed their distinctive *human* mental capacities and potentials.

There is now general agreement that human beings evolved as hunter-gatherers. And it was during this evolutionary period that as a species humans developed their enormous increase in brain size. There is still considerable debate and controversy over the precise length of this period (for details, see Whiten 1999). Some estimates, based on the discovery of stone tools, suggests that the hunter-gatherer period started about 2 million years ago. Such tools could, however, have been used for scavenging rather than genuine hunting. A more recent and perhaps more reliable estimate (one based on the discovery of spears fashioned with a balance similar to modern javelins) dates hunter-gathering back to some 400,000 years ago.

An important question here, of course, is how did such people live? A recent detailed ethnographic study of 24 living hunter-gatherer societies from four continents has searched for universal behaviour patterns which reflect the most fundamental forms of adaptation evolved by such groups during humans' evolution within their ancestral hunting niche (Erdal and Whiten 1996). The argument is that human species *became* human species as hunter-gatherers. We must be very cautious about extrapolating from modern-day groups to their equivalents in our evolutionary past. Earlier hunter-gatherers had smaller brains, and it could be that modern societies have been affected by more advanced agricultural societies. On the other hand, these studies may provide important insights into pre-modern practices and social relations. Most importantly, they consistently suggest that egalitarian behaviour, or a type of primitive communism, is indeed one of their most central and consistent features.

As we have earlier seen Maryanski and Turner suggesting, within such social groups there is a general absence of a permanent social hierarchy and a sharing of resources which goes well beyond the sharing that might be expected between kin or as a result of simple reciprocation. It is very difficult, however, to share Maryanski and Tuner's conclusion that these societies and the people within them are necessarily 'individualistic'. Active efforts are made within such societies to limit those individuals attempting to get more than their share of resources and power. The precise ways in which such egalitarian predispositions are realized or enforced vary considerably between cultures. (At their most extreme, they even include the killing the individuals involved.) But Maryanski and Turner's work does not provide any convincing evidence and, as outlined above, empirical work on existing hunter-gatherers does suggest that the collective and communal sharing of resources and power is a very common feature of human behaviour. The question remains, however, whether it is a universal characteristic of our evolved human nature, or of what Marx called our 'species-being'.

If (and the word 'if' remains important) pre-modern societies were characterized by communalism and sharing, they raise what has been called the 'egalitarian puzzle' (Knauft 1991). Chimpanzees are our closest living relatives. They are the primates with whom we share our most recent common ancestor of about 6 million years before the present. Bearing in mind that chimpanzees were and still are characterized by hierarchies of dominance, why should hominids start developing these more egalitarian predispositions? The answer according to this literature (sometimes categorized as 'cognitive ethology') is now increasingly being seen as an evolutionary one. According to this view, the answer lies less in culture, as Maryanski and Turner suggest, and more in our biologically evolved predispositions. Such mental, bodily and behavioural propensities evolved by our early ancestors enabled them, it is argued, to become effective hunter-gatherers. Therefore human beings adapted in ways which reduced conflict and maximized social harmony in the interests of survival. Food sharing would have reduced the risk for all individuals. It overcame variations in the returns from hunting. Animals typically kill more than they can eat at any one time. A group of animals which engaged in the planned and cooperative sharing of food, by contrast, increased the chances of each individual being adequately fed. According to this view, therefore, these early humans were primitive communists. But there is no need to romanticize such behaviour. An evolved collaboration in resource use can be seen as simply a very effective response to the problem of survival and reproduction.

A predisposition to counter permanent dominance can also be seen as conferring a distinct evolutionary advantage. Such societies are characterized by a division of labour which is based on skills, including those of hunting. But the argument is that a hunter would not be attributed a permanent position of power solely on the grounds of being a good hunter. A better evolutionary strategy than outright competition between individuals in hunter-gatherer society would be to allow those who are best at being hunters to act as the best hunters. As Erdal and Whiten (1996: 147) put it:

> Instead of wasting time and energy in a futile effort to dominate others, individuals who devoted enough of their personal resources to counteracting others' dominance, but did not waste time and energy by themselves trying to achieve dominance, would be able to devote much more energy to productive foraging and social behaviour. Those who remained trapped in the old dominance/submission patterns would be wasting their time by comparison.

Encephalization and the resulting great expansion in mental capacities (features which may have resulted from other processes such as the rise in hunting skills) have, according to these authors, been gradually turned to advantage. They have been used to replace primitive competitive behaviour based on physical superiority with forms of social expertise, cooperation, political alliances and what the literature on monkeys and apes calls 'Machiavellian intelligence' (see Humphrey 1976; Byrne 1995; Byrne and Whiten 1988; Whiten and Byrne 1997; Erdal and Whiten 1996; Whiten 1999). Intellects and an increasing consciousness of self are not only used, however, by individuals to think through and evaluate alternative courses of action. They are deployed to consider other minds, to project individuals' awareness of their own selves on to others. They are thereby used not just to solve problems but to bear in mind similar skills within other individuals. Such skills can be used outwit others, to deceive them, to detect deceit, to understand others' motives and manipulate them. As Ridley (1994: 33) puts it:

> There is an old story of a philosopher who runs when a bear charges him and his friend. 'It's no good, you'll never outrun a bear', says the logical friend. 'I don't have to', replies the philosopher, 'I only have to outrun you.'

In short, these distinctive capacities were evolved in social circumstances. The development of such consciousness of self and of others would have conferred an important adaptive advantage to our ancestors. And arguably, though this is not emphasized by the literature under review here, they could also have been used to build and reinforce bonds with others of their species

So Humphrey, Byrne, Whiten and others are arguing that our nearest ancestors developed skills and forms of adaptation which have developed towards that evolved by humans. 'Machiavellian intelligence', they suggest, further increased skills and brain power amongst our evolutionary ancestors, and this process, they argue, later evolved into the kinds of egalitarianism associated with hunter-gatherers and with modern human beings. It became, frankly, uneconomic to dominate. Survival, longevity and reproductive success were best guaranteed by collaboration. In these ways, to use Whiten's words, 'Machiavellian intelligence begot Egalitarianism, despite the gulf between them' (personal communication).

Finally, it is worth mentioning some of the implications of this work for the theory of evolution itself. Perhaps it suggests that humans have built into themselves an unconscious recognition of the needs of a group rather than the individual self. Similarly, it might suggest a genetically inherited motivation to cooperate and satisfy the group's needs rather than that of the individual. All this might imply that the unfashionable idea of selection having worked on differences between groups rather than on differences between individuals should be taken far more seriously (Wynne-Edwards 1986; Bendall 1998; Sober 1999).

Erdal and Whiten's overall thesis is summed up by Figure 1. It shows the shifts between hierarchical and egalitarian social structures over evolutionary time. Point A, at 6 million years before the present, is where the hominid line split from that of chimpanzees. As we can see, such early societies were typically characterized by social hierarchy. Point C represents the beginning of modern complex societies about 10,000 years ago. This is the point of the fall into hierarchy. And this stage in human history is constituted by the rise of pastoralism rather than the development of individualism and capitalism. Point B is where the beginnings of egalitarian social behaviour occurred with modern-day hunter-gatherers. As discussed earlier, it is not clear precisely when point B occurred but it is known that the period from B to C is sufficiently long for significant levels of evolution to have occurred and indeed for us to have evolved *as* human beings with our enormously increased brain size. As Erdal and Whiten (1996: 141) put it: 'If there are specific inherited predispositions for social behaviour, it must have been during this period that they were shaped by evolutionary processes.'

So, if this more recent research and the interpretations put on it by Erdal and Whiten are right, modern human beings emerged

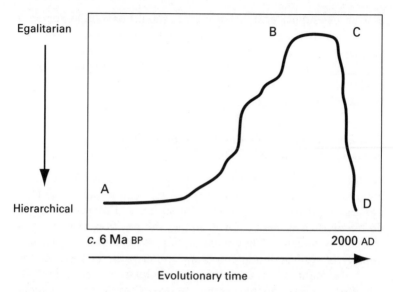

Figure 1 Social structure and human evolution (after Erdal and Whiten 1996)

from the very long period of evolutionary development when humans and their earlier relatives were adapting to simple forms of foraging societies (for a similar argument in the context of environmental conservation, see Rohe 1997). And coming to the more recent past, we now have hierarchical societies which (because there has been no time for significant biological evolution to occur) are thoroughly out of step with the types of humans which inhabit them.

This, then, is another version of the thesis we have encountered in a number of forms in this study, one which asserts that evolved human beings are now unsynchronized with their society. If the work of Whiten and his colleagues is right we are now living in and reproducing a set of circumstances which seem broadly in line with Kropotkin's account. The picture is the complete opposite of that offered by Maryanski and Turner. We have humans who are essentially collective and communal in a society which systematically mistreats and wrecks these predispositions. There remains, however, the question, one unasked by Erdal and Whiten and indeed by other authors making similar assertions, why it should be that an essentially egalitarian species should have constructed a society which is apparently so divorced from its own needs and propensities. Is this simply because a particularly dominant group of people have successfully imposed a society on the population as a whole? Or does this problem suggest that there is something wrong with this theory?

Humans as a collectively-orientated species in a hierarchical society? An evaluation

At this stage some further serious words of caution must be entered. First we must remain very careful about making 'golden age' assumptions about pre-modern societies. Erdal and Whiten do not outline in detail, for example, the position of women in these early societies. They mention in passing, however, that in a number of studies of contemporary hunter-gatherer societies the successful hunters' largess with meat helps them as individuals 'obtain the most capable women as wives' while offering more opportunities for adultery. It is difficult to know what to make of this. It could perhaps still be in line with a picture of hunter-gatherer societies which suggests these societies' essential egalitarianism also led to women's productive and reproductive roles being highly valued as part of a division of labour that was necessary for survival. In some instances, this does indeed seem to be the case. At the same time it could imply that the picture of dispersed and fluctuating power which Erdal and Whiten offer applies particularly to males and that females have been forced into a marginalized position. This, despite the fact that they are often economically more important in the sense that gathering usually brings in more calories per year than does hunting. In general, however, the recent egalitarian literature on hunter-gatherer societies mostly deals with lack of *male* hierarchies. It has not taken on board the more speculative but perhaps accurate and dialectical assertion of Bookchin to the effect that divisions of labour that were once valued and based on sharing became in due course made into fairly permanent and repressive regimes.

Second, the resulting psychologies or behavioural dispositions within modern human beings are surely likely to be complex and even contradictory. On the one hand, as discussed, there may be strong and dominant evolved predispositions in modern humans to resist domination, to share, to defer to others with superior skills and to perhaps remain confident of their own skills. These practices were, as Wilkinson (1997) puts it, 'basic to survival and to the quality of life'. On the other hand there could well remain predispositions to look after oneself, to protect oneself by hoarding or even stealing and killing. Thus, bearing in mind that modern human beings share a common ancestor with chimpanzees and apes with predispositions 'to dominate where possible', there may well remain predispositions stemming from our ancestral heritage and the older parts of the evolved brain. Studies of chimpanzees, gorillas and orang-utans are reminders of this heritage. Like humans, they lead a generally peaceful and harmonious life. On the other hand there remain well-documented occasions when they seek out, attack and kill members of their own species. Such behaviour is given special emphasis by Wrangham and Peterson (1997) in their 'demonic male' argument.

In short, it may well not be good enough to attribute those human practices we do not like to society and those that we do to 'human nature'. And indeed this more complex view of an evolved human nature, one which recognizes the possibility of *overlaid* egalitarian *and* individualistic and Machiavellian propensities within human beings, is briefly touched on by Maryanski and Turner, whose work was criticized above. More substantially, MacLean (1983, 1990) has even suggested that the human brain could take a 'triune' form, with three basic parts recapitulating our evolution. According to him there is a 'reptilian' core to the human brain, one composed of basic and self-serving survival instincts. This is surrounded by a 'paleomammalian' brain, which endowed our ancestors with a new set of predispositions, including an emergent affection for offspring. Finally, MacLean envisages a 'neomammalian' part of the brain, one which is linked with the emergence of reasoning, language and perhaps a degree of affection for people beyond blood family. In these ways, therefore, the human brain can be seen as the complex product of our evolutionary trajectory. According to this argument it is possible that humans have evolved as a sharing, sociable species. But at the same time there has remained a weaker ape element in our make-up (the 'old Adam') as well as a hunter-gather element ('man before the fall').

MacLean's three-layer picture is almost certainly too neat and mechanistic. More importantly, it may be attributing far too much to our evolutionary heritage. But it does at least indicate that modern human beings could be individualistic *and* egalitarian, solitary *and* sociable. His picture suggests a more complex position, one recently suggested by Boehm (1997) in an ongoing debate over the egalitarian thesis. He sees the unproblematic assertion of humans' egalitarian nature as contestable. In his view it is an unstable compromise between egalitarian 'control-from-below' and despotic domination-from-above:

> I do not think it is profitable to try and characterise human nature as being 'egalitarian' or 'despotic' or 'peaceful' or 'warlike', even though such labels make for lively debate. It is far more likely that our nature is many faceted and internally contradictory, and that political behaviour often involves a trade-off between dispositions that work in opposition in certain contexts.
>
> (Boehm 1997: 359)

We should note here an interesting contrast with Maryanski and Turner. Boehm sees modern democracy as controlling or keeping a lid on these tensions and contradictions. Democracy is therefore not, as *The Social Cage* suggests, allowing our latent individualism to be recognized. It is precisely the opposite; an attempt by dominant classes to control those who are attempting to understand and run their own lives. In the context of continuing forms of class, race and gender oppression, democracy (in the form of citizens' rights, the right to vote and so on) offers only a partial realization of individuals' capacities. A more jaundiced view of democracy of this kind is closer to the position of the two authors at the centre of this discussion, Marx and Bookchin.

Boehm's more general critique suggests that the original egalitarian thesis may be a considerable oversimplification as regards our biologically inherited nature. It could suggest multiple and perhaps conflicting propensities *within* the human genetic inheritance. These could coexist in dynamic tension. Maybe there is indeed one set of potentials towards sharing and communality and that these remain for the most part dominant. They have, after all, been a result of between half a million and 2 million years of our evolution. But another possibility is that there is a very diverse range of behaviour outcomes which stem from an underlying similarity in human predispositions. It is towards this position that we now work.

A way forward? Marx on human nature

While Marx never developed a systematic theory of human nature and of the relations between humans and nature, he made some important and increasingly influential speculations on this topic. At least part of his analysis may offer a way forward out of the impasse whereby humans are seen as either inherently collective and communal or individualistic and competitive.

Marx argued, first, for a fusion between naturalism and humanism. On the one hand he insisted that human beings are a natural sort. They are a part of nature, they are the product of evolution and their dispositions are a product of such biological development. On the other hand they are capable of becoming autonomous and making their own natures, futures and societies. Nevertheless, this fusion took different forms in different parts of his writings.

In *The Economic and Philosophical Manuscripts* Marx comes close to what might be termed the Kropotkinian view of human nature and indeed the view emerging from the work on humans' 'Machiavellian intelligence'. He argued that contemporary society actually denies the conditions for human emancipation. The division of labour, private property, industrialism and false consciousness all contribute to contemporary alienation rather than emancipation. Marx's dialectic applied to the relationship between the individual and society. Human beings, he argued, are essentially social. This essential sociality is part of their 'species-being', an element (along with their creative and linguistic capacities) which defines them as human beings. Identity and potential are therefore developed, fulfilled or denied in the context of the particular societies in which they are living and working. Thus human beings' potential to gain a full understanding of their relations with nature (one which, according to Marx, is unique to humans) remains unrealized in the type of capitalist society which humans have made.

Here, therefore, we find a strong normative concept of human nature, one which features high levels of optimism (Marx 1975a). Humans here are viewed as not only communal and collectively-orientated but having such inbuilt capacities as a strong aesthetic sense. These latent potentials are to be valued and are very much worth unlocking or 'unfolding':

> Only through the objectively unfolded wealth of human nature can the wealth of subjective human sensitivity – a musical ear, an eye for

beauty of form, in short, senses capable of human gratification – be
either cultivated or created.

(Marx 1975a: 353)

But Marx argues that contemporary society (and capitalist society
in particular, with its institution of private property, its very
advanced divisions of labour, the oppression of the state and its
many forms of false consciousness) has failed to unlock these
human essences and has turned human beings into egoistic, unfeel-
ing and destructive monsters. To put this another way, their nega-
tive characteristics will be changed once they live in a different kind
of (communist) society.

But in *Concerning Feuerbach*, originally written at about the
same time, Marx (1975b) wrote that 'the human essence is no
abstraction inherent in each single individual. In its reality it is the
ensemble of the social relations'. This view has some similarities
with G.H. Mead's (1934) insistence that the self arises from a
social process entailing interaction with other individuals. At
first reading it looks much more like mere description and not
much more than the Sartrean view that there is no human essence
at all (Poster 1979). It is a view of human nature as 'underdeter-
mined'. On the other hand, there is the implication here that given
a different 'ensemble of social relations' (as, for example, under
some form of communism) a distinctly different kind of human
essence could be forged. People remake themselves in the process
of forming and living in particular types of society. Similarly,
thinking about changing society necessarily means thinking about
what kinds of humans we wish to be. But this apparently more
neutral view of human nature also strongly suggests that what
Marx called 'the human essence' is adaptable to the particular
kinds of society, and the particular kinds of ecological niches,
which humans have made for themselves. Such flexibility has, in
Darwinian terms, given them an enormous advantage over other
species.

Finally, in *Capital* Marx offers a view which comes somewhere
between these two views. It can be seen as a combination of the two.
And it is this which seems the more productive way forward. On the
one hand Marx incorporated in his later work an idea of an invariant human nature which cannot be changed. At the same time he
recognizes that the particular ways in which invariant capacities are
realized, or fail to be realized, depend on the particular conditions

which they both encounter and make. As Marx put it in Volume 1 of *Capital*:

> If one wants to judge all human acts, movements, relations etc. in accordance with the principles of utility one must first deal with human nature in general and then with human nature as modified in each historical epoch.
>
> (Marx 1976, cited by Markovic 1991: 246)

The literature reviewed in this chapter converges on the fact that humans have the remarkably developed capacity for abstraction, for detached reflection on their own and on other beings' actions, motives and feelings. Self-reflection, the recognition of the self *by* the self, is an integral part of such abstraction, as are the formulation of goals and the capacity for communicating complex concepts to others. All these capacities constitute what Marx called 'human nature in general'. But how these powers actually work out (the forms, for example, of the actual abstractions people develop, the type of identity the adopt and recognize) depends on particular social and 'historical epochs' (Hirst 1994). Furthermore, there is no reason to suppose that the ideas people hold and communicate are necessarily either individualistic or communally-orientated. However, as the following chapter will suggest in more detail, this naturally inherited capacity for reflection and abstraction in relation to practical activity is by no means evenly realized by all members of society. More specifically, these natural human endowments are both promoted and denied in a modern capitalist society. Some classes of people are realizing the full range of their capacities but meanwhile others, as a result of various forms of social domination, are having their capacities unrealized. As I hope to show, it is from this point that an alternative kind of 'social Darwinism' can start to be constructed. It is a 'social Darwinism from below', one which combines elements of modern evolutionary thought with an understanding of the class and other power relations constituting modern society.

6

Social Darwinism: Towards a New Synthesis

This final chapter outlines a possible new relation between evolutionary and social thought, one which avoids the dualisms and reductionisms discussed in earlier chapters and the implicit prejudices of the earliest forms of social Darwinism. It also avoids the kinds of analogizing which have formed such a large part of evolutionary thought in the social sciences. Drawing on recent developments in biology, epidemiology and health psychology, it discusses possible future directions for research on the relations between capitalism and human evolution.

The chapter has three elements. It first re-emphasizes those forms of developmental biology which concentrate on the organism rather than on genetics. Second, it is concerned with the impact of capitalism on the human organism. The power relations of modern society result in conceptual work and knowledge being highly prized and allocated to some people, while practical work and knowledge are downgraded and allocated to others. But the concentration of power and control in modern society is not unproblematic. It also brings serious health problems. Third, and using recent developments in the life sciences, the chapter speculates on possible long-term relations between capitalism, ontogeny and human evolution. This raises some important implications for future forms of politics. Is capital now reconstructing human biology in its own image?

Organism-centred views of human development

The biological tradition developed here concentrates on the genetically-based potential of organisms for a flexible interaction with their environment. As we will later see, it also raises the possibility of long-term *self*-evolution and organization. Such a position draws on, and is a fusion of, a long-emergent biology and 'biological psychology' represented by authors from both biology and psychology. We encountered this perspective in Chapters 3 and 5 (see also Baldwin 1902; Waddington 1957, 1975; Piaget 1971; Lewontin 1982, 1991; Gottlieb 1992; Bidell and Fischer 1997; Robertson 1999).

There are several common elements to this alternative approach. Again, genes are downplayed as causal mechanisms and considered as reproducing, and indeed changing, real causal powers and *potentials* for both the development and stability of organisms. Genes interact in many and complex ways with one another, with cells, with organisms and even with the external environment. Behaviour and development are definitely not reduced to genes and genetic structure (Ho 1998).

The work of Piaget, partly based on that of Waddington, is one obvious place to start making links between evolutionary thought on the one hand and social relations and processes on the other. According to Piaget, human beings' biologically programmed early development entails a series of stages in early childhood from 'pre-operational' to 'concrete operational' reasoning at around 8 years – 'concrete' because they are still linked to objects (classifying things, putting them in series, noting connections, understanding numbers) (Piaget 1971: 17). This results, from about the age of 11, in an increased capacity to coordinate various pieces of information, to draw general conclusions from diverse pieces of information and to combine thought with action and engage in 'reversibility' between actions and thoughts – thinking around a problem and using means to ends.

According to Piaget, the first developmental stage lasts from birth up until the age of about 2. This is the 'sensorimotor' stage in which children are learning from their senses, by touching and feeling objects and physically exploring their environment. The 'pre-operational' stage, lasting from about age 2 to about 7, is one

in which children acquire mastery of language and start using words
to represent objects and images in a symbolic way. However, they
still have little capacity for understanding general concepts. Their
capacities for reasoning are limited. They will not understand, for
example, that if water is poured from a tall, thin, container into a
shorter wider one, the volume of water is the same, despite the fact
that the water level is lower (the so-called 'conservation test'). As
the child develops into the 'concrete operational stage' (during the
ages of 7–11) he or she becomes able to understand abstract and
logical notions and draw general conclusions. False reasoning over
the containers and the water is overcome. Mathematical operations
such as multiplying and dividing become possible. In the 'formal
operational stage', covering the ages of 11–16, the capacity for
grasping abstract and hypothetical ideas becomes further developed.

The result (assuming all goes well) is a shift away from a logic
based solely on instinctive and immediate responses and, by stages,
towards knowledge of the world and, eventually, the development
of a capacity to grasp, use and communicate rational and abstract
ideas. Note, however, that *both* such capacities and understandings
remain combined within the organism, the living human being.
Piaget was at pains to point to the increasing differentiation-cum-
integration of the completed brain. He attempted to overcome the
dualism outlined earlier by arguing that other animals also have
learning capacities and brains which act in a coordinating, central-
izing way.

Early development is still given special prominence by biologists
and psychologists now emphasizing whole organisms rather than
genes *per se*. But recent work within this tradition suggests that the
mental development of an individual (more specifically the organization of their nerve cells) depends partly on genetic inheritance but
also on information acquired during development. As Richardson
(1998: 70) puts it: 'The microcircuitry of the cortex (the most
recently evolved part of the brain in mammals) is "wired up" only
in a rudimentary fashion at birth, with functional development
dependent on actual experience.'

This raises a major question mark over Piagetian assumptions that
individual development is universal and hard-wired. This is a matter
to which we will return. For now we should recognize the 'developmental plasticity' of the brains of humans. This again points to the

reciprocal interaction between organisms and environment. On the one hand mental structures are 'experience-expectant' – designed, that is, to develop or unfold neural mechanisms in relation to experience. On the other hand, brains are 'experience-dependent' – storing information which is unique to an individual and holding it until it is released by an external event (Greenhough *et al.* 1993; see also Fischbach 1992; Shatz 1992; Robertson 1999). Presumably genes for such developmental plasticity were, like other genes, selected for by standard evolutionary processes.

This type of work then points to the evolved *potential* of developing human beings. We will return to this kind of perspective when we return to Piaget. The problem is, however, that it still does not adequately explain the actual processes by which human beings came to develop their very considerable mental capacities in relation to their environment. Wills argues for a feedback loop in which individuals with better brains interacted with their physical and linguistic environment to make it more complex. But more complex environments have in turn, he believes, selected in favour of individuals with better brains: 'Big and clever brains led to more complex cultures and bodies suited to take advantage of them, which in turn led to yet bigger and cleverer brains' (Wills 1993: xxii).

There is now, however, a great deal of palaeontological literature suggesting that the early apes from which we are descended did not develop their immense mental structures simply by thinking up new and better ideas (Woods and Grant 1995). Rather, they developed their very advanced mental capacities through *interacting* with the world in a physical sense, working on it, making tools, communicating about it and, more generally, both adapting and evolving in relation *to* their environment. But this leaves open what we mean by 'environment'. Bearing this in mind, we now turn to capitalism and its possible interactions with the human species' capacities.

Power, capitalism and the fragmentation of human capacities

Historical materialism insists that at the core of a society is the mode of production, the way in which human societies organize to work on nature and produce the things they need (Cohen 1978). Human societies therefore interact with ecological systems and with other organisms in all sorts of ways, but it is the mode of production, the ways of appropriating the materials and powers of nature which remain central to a historical materialist account (Martinez Allier 1987; O'Connor 1994; Benton 1996b). Modes of production, and in particular the relationships made between people in the labour process, therefore dominate the way in which social formations as a whole interact with nature – internal as well as external.

People, as we have seen Piaget arguing, possess the potential for abstract reasoning and are capable of combining such thinking with the more intuitive type of understanding which they acquired in early childhood. But how do these potentials fare in a capitalist mode of production? Piaget's work has been criticized for not adequately covering the developing human's relation to its environment, to both the natural and the social worlds (Butterworth *et al.* 1998). This is a criticism which is particularly apposite to the argument being mounted here. Piaget tended to ignore social context and to overemphasize fixed-length stages determined by a child's innate capacities. But these are not feasible propositions. Young children already have well-developed skills before coming to school and their skills for abstract thought are brought out, or realized, by the particular social context in which they develop. In particular, they are more likely to develop their thinking in situations with which they can identify and where their own and other people's intentions are clear. 'These human intentions', Donaldson (1978: 121) argues, 'are the matrix in which the child's thinking is embedded'. The development of human beings therefore needs seeing in the context of their interaction with other human minds and physical objects.

Similarly, Buck-Morss (1982) points to the importance of context. She argues that Piagetian psychology is 'impregnated with explicit as well as implicit assumptions about the nature of man (including his cognitive functioning) from a Western point of view' (Buck-Morss 1982: 276). She detects a value-judgement whereby formal thinking is in some sense 'better' than concrete thinking. She argues, therefore, that this type of psychology consciously or unconsciously asserts the values of Western capitalist society in which abstract knowledges can be bought and sold. There is much to be gained from Buck-Morss's argument. It again suggests that Piagetian theory, important as it remains, underestimates the combination of modern capitalist societies with humans' innate capacities, in particular the promotion of abstract thought by capitalism. She cites research which shows, for example, that children in Western industrialized societies are quickest to grasp abstract and logical structures separated from context, and that children in non-Western societies are more likely to able to deal with the 'conservation test' if pottery is made by their families. An understanding of underlying causal powers and types of individual development therefore needs combining with the contingencies of particular kinds of social relations (for further discussion, see Miller 1997; Sylva 1997).

This brings us to a key point in this attempt to combine evolutionary thought with social theory. A central feature of capitalism, and its state-capitalist variants, has been its long-term tendency to separate more abstract thought from more intuitive and experiential forms of thinking. Furthermore, these different kinds of activity tend to be allocated to different groups of people. Why should this be so? Separate groups of people whose role was to develop and communicate abstract ideas are not unique to capitalism. (In ancient Egypt, for example, there was a priestly caste whose role was to do mathematics.) As we will see, however, under capitalism the process has been made into a central element in managing social relations and labour processes. Knowledge which is embedded in practice and context tends to be further undervalued and denigrated (Hales 1980). What Hegel called 'immediate' thought is thereby constantly disabled through lack of linkage to more abstract forms of knowledge.

Battles over knowledge have long been a central feature of social change. But developments during the late eighteenth and early nineteenth centuries were particularly important (Drouin and Bensaude-Vincent 1996; Outram 1996; Secord 1996; Shteir 1996). It was at this point that popular scientific knowledge started to be radically segregated from the science of the laboratory or field-station. Popular knowledge was made increasingly secondary. Shteir (1996: 151), referring to the early nineteenth century, for example, writes:

> Practitioners, 'gentlemen of science,' hobbyists, writers and public lecturers reflected in various ways a growing bifurcation in science culture. As in other aspects of nineteenth-century culture, there was a deepening divide between the general and the specialist, the popular and the academic, between the 'high' science of gentlemen in metropolitan

learned societies and the 'low' science of practitioners who diffused
scientific knowledge for practical use.

Such separation was again accompanied by the marginalization
of the knowledge acquired by, for example, women and artisans as
well as other dedicated amateurs such as clergymen. This despite
the fact that the development of abstract ideas depended on evidence collected by non-experts. It has even been suggested that
Darwin himself was the last to combine a life of observation and
experience with one based on theory (Outram 1996). Yet it is easy
to romanticize practical understanding. Remember that early naturalism was closely aligned with mysticism and religion. In Comte's
terms it still belonged to the earliest 'theological' stage in social
evolution. As Barber (1980: 25) writes:

> Science counted for absolutely nothing compared to religion. Time
> and again in popular handbooks we find the writer asking 'Why does
> such-and-such occur?' and then answering himself with pious evasion,
> 'Because God ordains it.'

But what were (and indeed still are) the underlying mechanisms
to these processes of fragmentation? The emerging power of
abstract knowledge can be partly attributed to the growth and
extent of 'commodity abstraction'. Much of life in capitalist society
is organized around abstraction. In particular, the buying and
selling of goods means that people are constantly obliged to think
in terms of an abstract substance known as 'value'. In this highly
important respect, everyday life for almost everyone entails continuous abstraction (Sohn-Rethel 1975). And this in turn involves
neglecting concrete details, not least details of the circumstances
under which goods are actually *made*. This links to a second key
process underlying abstraction.

Historical materialism places particular stress on the social relations surrounding the production process and the marginalization
of knowledge which accompanies the exercise of class power. In
particular, it directs our attention to the ways in which a subordinated working class is deskilled in the process of paid work. Capital
takes up general knowledge as a force of production. On the one
hand, as Marx put it in *Grundrisse*, '[t]he accumulation of knowledge and skill, of the productive power of society's intelligence, is
absorbed into capital in opposition to labour' (cited in McLellan
1977: 377). Meanwhile, the division of labour 'converts the labourer

into a crippled monstrosity', using his or her capacity for manual dexterity but ignoring her or his other capacities 'just as in the States of La Plata they butcher a whole beast for the sake of his hide or his tallow' (cited in McLellan 1977: 477)

More generally, we should turn to Volume 1 of *Capital*, where Marx's theory of the formal and the real subsumption of labour to capital is laid out. The 'formal' process refers to 'the direct subordination of the labour to capital, irrespective of the state of its technological development' (Marx 1976: 1034). 'Real' subsumption refers to the full-scale transformation of the labour processes and relations of production under particular social and technological conditions. Real subsumption means the workers lose their autonomy. Their work is reduced to following the movements of the capitalist's machine.

Marx's original analysis of 'deskilling' has now been considerably developed (see, for example, Braverman 1974; Hales 1980). Deskilling in the sphere of paid work is perhaps best seen as taking knowledges out of a given labour process and placing them in the possession of a materially distinct set of workers sometimes known as 'mental' workers. But once such transfer has taken place the knowledge can be transformed and embodied in new labour processes. Mechanization is the classic form of this process. Despite later modifications of Marx's theory, however, 'formal' and 'real' subsumption can still be seen as a central feature of modern social relations.

Recent feminist and feminist-inspired analysis has been particularly prominent in showing how modern science has continued to both separate and marginalize practical, lay and localized understandings in areas other than paid work. Lambert and Rose (1996), for example, have outlined the difficult relationships between situated and disembodied knowledges in contemporary medical practice. A similar point is made by feminist activists in developing countries where the denial and overriding by powerful vested interests of local ecological knowledge and the skills of women continues apace. Mies and Shiva (1993) show that the separation and subordination of certain types of work and knowledge extends to home and community. Certain types of knowledge and labour are again categorized as merely passive and uncreative. The teaching of important social learning skills to the developing child are, for example, marginalized as a mere prelude to learning 'real' knowledge relevant to the supposedly more authentic sphere of paid work. Meanwhile, such subordination has been compounded by Marxian analysis. Historical materialism, as implied, has long ignored the unpaid skills of people (especially those of women) for raising children and conducting other forms of domestic work.

The combination of insights from historical materialism with those from writers such as Piaget shows that the 'the politics of knowledge' is not 'political' simply in terms of denying human beings' inbuilt skills for linking situated knowledge to more abstract ideas. It is also central to exercising control over certain groups of people. But does the subdivision of human potentials apply to dominant as well as dominated classes? Much less so, since these people are in a better position to see and manipulate the connections between different types of knowledge. Social elites are thereby able to maintain a distinctive overall understanding and control of their own circumstances and, of course, the circumstances of other people.

Capitalism: a third contradiction

However, the exertion of power (through the management of knowledge and in more obvious and coercive forms) is by no means problem-free. Marx asserted that the fundamental contradiction in capitalism was that between social production and private appropriation for the enhancement of particular interests. More recent 'green' forms of Marxism emphasize a second contradiction, that between capitalist production relations and the 'external physical conditions' of such relations – damage to ecosystems, the ozone layer, non-human species and so on (Benton 1996a). But a third contradiction is that between capital and *internal* nature – the capacity of people to remain healthy and work productively. As Marx (cited in McLellan 1977: 478) put it: 'Capital is reckless of the health or length of life of the labourer, unless under compulsion from society'.

The material well-being of people in advanced industrial societies has clearly undergone massive improvements. In Liverpool in 1840, for example, the average age of death was 35 for professional people, 22 for tradespeople and their families and 15 for labourers. Today, male life expectancy in Britain is 74. These are the real gains. But modern industrial capitalism continues to be 'reckless'. The subtle degradation of human health resulting from very large numbers of synthetic compounds is one example (Colborn *et al.* 1996). Another is the emergence of what James (1997) calls 'the low serotonin society', a society engaged in excessive individualism, status anxiety, unstable social attachments and an all too ready supply of antidepressants.

A more subtle yet pervasive form of recklessness concerns the link between inequality and health. Of course inequality is hardly unique to capitalism so it is not clear that capitalism *per se* causes ill health. It is clear, however, that different versions of capitalism, and the different levels of inequality they incorporate, can exacerbate or improve people's well-being.

A general association between social inequality and poor health is a well-known feature of medical sociology. It has become a central starting-point for much of contemporary public health policy (Townsend and Davidson 1980; Whitehead 1987). And the links between absolutely poverty and poor health are clear enough when we consider the millions of people in Africa, India and South America who eat badly, drink unclean water and live in insanitary shanty towns. Average life expectancy sub-Saharan Africa, for example, is 52 years. In India it is 58 years. Contrast this with 75 years in the developed capitalist societies (World Bank 1993).

However, contemporary work on the relationship between income and health in Western societies adds two new twists to the argument. It suggests that power relations and *relative* inequalities are creating real problems. This literature therefore strongly suggests that health is more likely to suffer within societies where inequalities of power take their most extreme forms. Life expectancy in countries with high levels of equality such as Sweden, Norway and the Netherlands is, for example, higher than it is in Britain and the USA (Wilkinson 1996, 1997). As Wilkinson (1997: 128) puts it:

> Living standards for the vast majority of people in the developed world have long surpassed the levels at which absolute material standards are the main limitation on health: what matters now is where your income places you in the social hierarchy.

But why should social inequality in relatively affluent societies link to decreased life expectancy and to more general health problems? Obvious factors such as eating badly and living in bad housing are again important, but other mechanisms seem to be at work. Essentially, we are seeing health deteriorating in societies where the differences in power relations are at their most extreme.

So what are the biological mechanisms involved? Humans, like most other animals, have evolved powerful responses when confronted by a physical, mental or emotional threat. Their bodies automatically respond by preparing themselves to stay and resist or to flee and capitulate. The processes involved are now becoming well understood. They include the release of sugar and fats into the bloodstream to provide fuel for quick energy, red blood cells flooding the bloodstream to carry more oxygen to the muscles of the limbs and brain, the heart beating faster, blood pressure rising and blood starting to clot in anticipation of injury (see, for example, Patel 1996).

More recent work shows that continued exposure to stressful circumstances can severely affect the body's immune system. The norm is for protective substances called antibodies to be made in order to protect us from foreign substances known as antigens. In addition, natural cells seek and out and destroy cells that have acquired foreign characteristics, such as infected or cancer cells. 'Stress' is a word containing a number of connotations (Selye 1984). On the one hand it can include elements of interest, engagement, involvement and determination. On the other hand, it includes elements of dissatisfaction, boredom, uncertainty, anxiety, alienation and, ultimately, an exceeding of the limits of endurance. Most importantly, researchers have consistently found that people repeatedly exposed to stressful circumstances undergo an impairment in these resistances (Seligman 1975).

These studies again show that lack of social power is a key reason for the link between inequality and bad health in Western societies. If people have little control over their lives their health begins to suffer. This is a picture confirmed by much contemporary research (see, for example, Brunner 1997; Martin 1997; Lovallo 1997). As Patel (1996: 13), another researcher working in this area, puts it:

> If such adaptive responses are prolonged, intense or frequently repeated, they increase wear and tear, exhaust the body of its adaptive energy and may eventually damage the structure and function of one or more organs in the body. The final effect may be serious illness of the body or the mind or even death.

And in a well-known study of British civil servants it was found that those with access to the least organizational power and control over their own work had by far the worst health (Brunner *et al.* 1996; Bosma *et al.* 1997). This includes, in particular, cardiovascular problems. One of the researchers involved in this study puts the matter as follows.

> There is clear evidence that the risk of cardiovascular disease in affluent societies rises sharply with decreasing occupational status, even among office-based workers who are not poor in the conventional sense, nor exposed to physical hazards.
>
> (Brunner 1996: 296)

So despite their generally rising levels of health, many human beings in contemporary society fall ill. This, then, is one well-documented result of extremes in power relations. But second, recent research also offers significant insights into how ill health is consistently passed on within families. The emphasis again shifts away from genes *per se* and towards the genetically-inherited propensities of human beings. How are these propensities affected by the kinds of societies in which they live?

Recent advances in epidemiology suggest, for example, that a pregnant mother gives an unwitting 'weather forecast' to her unborn child, signalling the kind of world into which he or she will be born (Barker 1998; Bateson and Martin 1999). Children from poorer backgrounds are thereby being designed to make the best of a bad job. Their blood-flow, metabolisms and production of hormones lead to altered bodily structures and functions. In harshly Darwinian terms, they are made well adapted to their environment, even if this environment is distinctly human-made. Similar processes of adaptation have been found in other species such as sheep, pigs and rats. A key result for humans is that they are more likely to suffer from illnesses such as chronic bronchitis and cardiovascular disease. Furthermore, their lives are likely to be shorter than the average. And very importantly, 'weather forecasts' appear to be passed on from one generation to the next, the capacity of a woman to nourish her foetus being in part determined by that woman's own intra-uterine experience. We can therefore begin to envisage a biological mechanism contributing to the continued reproduction of an 'unfit' underclass; generations of people being not only born into poor circumstances but constructed for such contexts and, furthermore, even passing on inherited biological misfortunes to their children. But, paradoxically, children also suffer if they are born into conditions to which they are *not* well adapted. If, for example, a child whose mother has been starved is born into a world with high levels of sugar in food this results in an increased predisposition to diabetes. Again, in Darwinian terms, we are witnessing the failure of those least 'fit' for their environment.

However, the significance of early development for later well-being is now seen as extending well beyond the pre-natal stage. There is now a fast-growing literature which shows that how a child is treated in infancy, childhood and adolescence strongly affects how he or she develops in later life (see, for example, Montgomery *et al.* 1996, 1997; Marmot and Wadsworth 1997; Keating and Herzman 1999). Thus emotional stability, educational performance, cognitive capacities and social mobility have all been demonstrated to be closely related to how a child is brought up in the home, school and wider society. This clearly places a large question mark over arguments that such capacities or incapacities are genetically hard-wired into the human population.

This work largely supplants attempts to explain well-being and intelligence simply in terms of either 'genes' or 'environment'. The argument now centres on development in context. Are discrete events in early life responsible for problems in adulthood? Or are such problems the productive of cumulative events during the life-course? Or are they, as we might expect, a combination of both such processes (Power and Hertzman 1999)?

We are now in a position to make some preliminary links between this important empirical work and forms of evolutionary thought, which so far remain rather unexplored, and forms of social theory which have also somewhat languished. In the latter case we are referring to Marx's theory of subsumption. Bringing these two areas of thought together enables us to ask a key question: is capitalism constructing human biology in its own image?

Biological-cum-social evolution: the subsumption of human biology?

What, then, of the relations between society and long-term human evolution? How are social change and the genetically-based development of human beings combining? Again, very little is known about the processes involved, but it is least theoretically possible that experiences undergone during individual develop-ment may produce longer-term evolutionary effects.

In line with Waddington's work, considerable emphasis is now given to the *adaptability* of organisms to environmental shocks, to underlying but unexpressed genetic potential in riding new shocks and to the growth of complexity, especially amongst birds and mammals, in dealing with changing environmental conditions. Responses to environmental change therefore realize so far un-realized capacities and potentials. The environment is selecting for genes as much as vice versa. And, most significantly, over a long period it is the adaptable that are selected for. This entails what Wills (1989) calls 'the wisdom of the genes' and what Richardson (1998) calls 'the remarkable degrees of developmental plasticity' in the brains of animals and humans (see also Robertson 1999). This can look teleological in the sense that it might seem as though there has all along been some underlying purpose to evolution. But the 'wisdom of the genes' argument is simply pointing to the relative flexibility and robustness of organisms (and perhaps particularly of the human organism) as a result of their evolutionary history.

Waddington used the metaphor of an 'epigenetic landscape' in which the developing organism is seen as developing within a set of genetically determined hills and valleys (Figure 2). The valleys rep-resent what he called the 'chreods' or 'necessary paths' which are different for each individual. A developing organism passes down these paths and, as the hill and valley metaphor implies, is not easily pushed from one chreod to another. The organism is relatively robust in this sense and returns to its original chreod so long as random genetic changes and environmental shocks are not too great. Small deviations do not, therefore, prevent a large number of children from developing towards similar endpoints. Bateson (1982: 394), referring to Waddington's picture, refers to '[t]he astonishing capacity of the developing system to right itself after a perturbation and return to its former track'.

Nevertheless, while stability and plasticity may be the norm, large perturbations generated by changing environments or genetic struc-tures may lead to a substantial shift in the form of a move to a differ-ent pathway or developmental outcome. Most importantly for Waddington (and for our assertions here) ontogenetic development

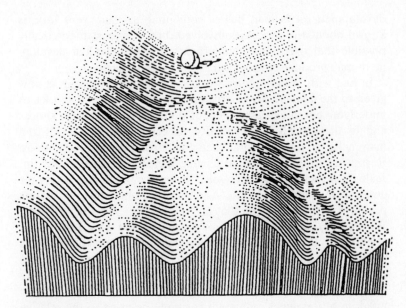

Figure 2   The epigenetic landscape
Source: Waddington 1975. Reproduced with kind permission of Edinburgh
University Press.

may well be having long-term evolutionary effects. Those individuals with suitable pathways are able to adapt, survive and leave
offspring. Over time, he argued, the population will develop in such
a way that a high number of its members will possess a set of chreods
that is better and more adapted to the new conditions. The 'epigenetic landscape' of the whole population is thereby altered in
response to its environment (Box 8).

In developing and applying such ideas, however, there again
remain a large number of unknowns. First, there may be difficulties
with Waddington's conclusions. The significance of the environment in his work is not entirely clear. If, for example, the population had two chreods, one leading to white flies and one leading
to black, and the environment changed so as to push the majority
of flies into growing up white, this would not necessarily lead to
selection in favour of flies for which the white chreod is more
prominent. Everything would depend on whether the environmental change also gave a selective advantage to white flies.
Perhaps Waddington got his results because his environmental

Box 8   Genetics and the flexibility of organisms: Waddington's experiments on fruitflies

With the aid of experiments with fruitflies, Waddington showed how environmental shocks led to a great new variability within a population. Such variability was a result of realizing the potential of large-scale *existing* genetic variation rather than the generation of major new genetic change. Within a few generations flies with the new characteristics were being produced without the shocks being administered. In these ways characteristics which had been inherited from the environment were being passed on to later generations. In this longer-term sense (and one which applied to large populations rather than individuals) acquired characteristics were inherited. This suggests that the genetic constitution of an organism is flexible – allowing, that is, the emergence of a number of physically and behaviourally distinct forms and behaviours, variations being partly or even largely dependent on environmental change. It also re-emphasizes the 'wisdom of the genes' argument, the close link between organism and environment and a rejection of the reductionist emphasis on organisms as simple 'expressions' of genes.

change happened to do both these things. But this would simply be a coincidence, and the fact that the environmental change led both to a first-generation change to characteristic x and to a change over several generations to a genetic predisposition to develop x would be a coincidence. In other words, this might not be a simple case of acquired characteristics being passed on to future generations.

One possible implication for humans of Waddington's work is that subpopulations could be developing their pre-existing genetically-based potentials in ways which allow them to be better adapted to the demands of a capitalist society. Have the forms of social domination outlined earlier after all been leading to the development of people with certain kinds of characteristic? Have we all along been witnessing the slow evolution of interbreeding, clannish social elites who have developed particularly well-enhanced capacities for handling and communicating abstract ideas? To put this in more theoretical terms, does the subsumption of labour to capital now include biologically-based capacities or even the gene pool? At the moment, it must be said, there is little evidence of a ruling class being created which has greater innate mental potential. As we saw in Chapter 4, early environment is especially important and the key predictor of adult IQ is the social class of one's mother. High levels of exogamy combined with growing numbers of *nouveaux riches* in a country such as Britain or the United States almost certainly mean that the ruling classes do not form a separate gene pool. Meanwhile, has interbreeding between subordinated classes of people been leading to large numbers of people being born with ill-developed mental potential? Again, the evidence does not exist and this can only be a question at this stage. Nevertheless, such forms of inheritance are still theoretically possible, even if they are not taking place on the scale suggested by Herrnstein and Murray (McGue 1997).

We must be clear what was being argued by Waddington. Passing on genetic characteristics to later generations may look like a process of Lamarckian evolution. But the word 'look' is important. Or, as Waddington (1975) argues, it is a version of Lamarckism not usually associated with Lamarck himself. It is simply that those with certain characteristics, including mental structures, will be enabled to thrive and pass on their distinctive characteristics to their progeny. However, some contemporary biologists do indeed go even further and suggest that characters acquired during an organism's lifetime actually can be inherited by future generations. The Weissman doctrine (asserting the continuity of the germ plasm and its rigid separation from the somatic cells of the body) turns out to be questionable (Jablonska and Lamb 1995). It is becoming increasingly clear that genetic events in somatic cells actually can have a direct effect on the germ line and hence on the inherited characters of the next generation. More recently, Ho (1998: 120) suggests, on the basis of recent research, that 'there is no longer any doubt that acquired characteristics are inherited in many different forms'. It seems, for example, that an acquired tolerance to foreign antigens can be inherited via the male line. Significantly, Ho (1998: 120–1) suggests that there are cellular mechanisms 'that effectively report back to the germline, to change the genes or to stabilise them according to the experiences of somatic cells' (see also Steele *et al.* 1998).

It must be strongly emphasized that the fusion between historical materialism and human evolution proposed earlier (one linking the developing organism to its content) does not depend on the Lamarckian and genetic mechanisms discussed above. Nevertheless, the work by Ho *et al.* implies that acquired characteristics could indeed be having some long-term evolutionary effects, that information can be transmitted to descendants in ways other than through the familiar base sequence of DNA. In recent years Lamarckism has been relegated merely to processes of *cultural* reproduction. Its application has been extended almost wholly to the realm of ideas (see, for example, Cavalli-Sforza and Feldman 1981; Barkow *et al.* 1992) But the kind of biology represented by Ho and others suggests that Lamarckian biology perhaps should not have been so rapidly dismissed.

Again, such arguments remain highly controversial. It is by no means clear precisely which characteristics are being transferred from one generation to the next. And, given the random nature of evolution, there is absolutely no guarantee that characteristics such as 'IQ' will be passed on at all. But this recent work from the natural sciences again points to a conceivable feedback on human evolution of social relations and practices.

These unconventional forms of biology-cum-sociology therefore remind us of not only *The Bell Curve* but also of Herbert Spencer and his Lamarckian argument that society evolves via the transmission of acquired and exercised human characteristics. But, even if there is a tendency for some genetically-based potentials to be passed on between classes of people in a Lamarckian fashion, the environment of course remains important. Whether these potentials are realized or repressed still critically depends on context – on family-support, schooling, welfare and a host of other social and cultural influences. Furthermore, we must remember the research outlined earlier, some of which suggested that a child might well 'acquire' before birth characteristics which are passed on to later generations. However, this is by no means the same thing as suggesting that such characteristics are directly attributable to genes.

The critique of capitalism proposed here is quite different from that in the first section of this chapter. It was argued there that capitalism might be denying certain people's capacities for creative and reflexive thought. At the same time, subordinated people may be subject to poor levels of health. But here the suggestion is that there could be a gradual embedding of a division between abstract and concrete thinking in the biological structure of the population. Such an assertion is a radical extension of Marx's theory of subsumption.

Over the next few decades the direct modification of foetuses will almost certainly take place. At first this will eliminate genes which predispose people to certain illnesses. Later the process may be extended to improve intelligence, looks, athleticism or whatever else people want for their offspring. Even now, wealthy American parents are engaging in a form of DIY eugenics, advertising for donors whose eggs are likely to produce children of high intelligence. Meanwhile, on the supply side, fashion photographer Ken Harris is advertising the eggs of models on the Internet. 'Every organism is evolving to its most perfect state', he argues. 'Finding traits that repair your genetic flaws is what we are all about' (Reeves 1999). The social, political and perhaps health implications of such developments are serious enough. But perhaps they are just part of a more general and longer-term process of 'real subsumption', one in which capital is modifying human biological structure in its own image. Marx (1976: 360) argued that workers' skills were becoming so diminished and their movements so subjected to the capitalist's machine that they had become 'by nature unfitted to make anything independently'. Perhaps this statement is more literally true than he realized.

The kind of 'social Darwinism' outlined here turns the arguments of *The Bell Curve* on their head. There could well be a biological basis to social polarization but, if capital has started to capture and modify the biological or even genetic structure of the human population, variations in human biology are by no means pure accident. The long-term social and political implications of such a development (as well as the implications for social and evolutionary theory themselves) are therefore just as significant as the theories propounded by either Herbert Spencer or Herrnstein and Murray. Capital, driven by the combination of increased scientific knowledge and the search for profits, is now actively reconstructing the biologies of non-human species. Whether and how capital reconstructs the biology of humanity (whether, that is, a merger is effected between social and human biological evolution) could become the central area of social and political conflict in the twenty-first century.

References

Alchian, A. (1950) 'Uncertainty, evolution and economic theory', *Journal of Political Economy*, 58, June, 211–22.

Andreasen, R. (1998) 'A new perspective on race', *British Journal for the Philosophy of Science*, 49(4), 199–225.

Ardrey, R. (1961) *African Genesis: A Personal Investigation into the Animal Origins and Nature of Man*. New York: Atheneum.

Aron, R. (1969) *Eighteen Lectures on Industrial Society*. London: Weidenfeld and Nicolson.

Baldwin, J. (1902) *Development and Evolution*. London: Macmillan.

Bannister, R. (1979) *Social Darwinism: Science and Myth in Anglo-American Social Thought*. Philadelphia: Temple University Press.

Barber, L. (1980) *The Heyday of Natural History 1820–1870*. London: Cape.

Barkan, E. (1992) *The Retreat of Scientific Racism: Changing Concepts of Race in Britain and the United States between the World Wars*. Cambridge: Cambridge University Press.

Barker, D. (1998) *Mothers, Babies and Health in Later Life*. London: Churchill Livingstone.

Barkow, J., Cosmides, L. and Tooby, J. (1992) *The Adapted Mind: Evolutionary Psychology and the Generation of Culture*. Oxford: Oxford University Press.

Bateson, P. (1982) 'Rules and reciprocity in behavioural development', in H. Plotkin (ed.) *Learning, Development and Culture*. Chichester: Wiley.

Bateson, P. and Martin, P. (1999) *Design For a Life: How Behaviour Develops*. London: Cape.

Beck, U. (1992) *The Risk Society*. London: Sage.

Bell, D. (1973) *The Coming of Industrial Society*. New York: Basic Books.

Bendall, K. (1998) 'For goodness sake, it's survival', *Financial Times*, 12 September.

Benton, T. (1991) 'Biology and social science: Why the return of the repressed should be given a (cautious) welcome', *Sociology*, 25(1): 1–29.

Benton, T. (ed.) (1996a) *The Greening of Marxism*. New York: Guilford Press.

Benton, T. (1996b) 'Marxism and natural limits: An ecological critique and reconstruction' in T. Benton (ed.) *The Greening of Marxism*. New York: Guilford Press.

Bidell, T. and Fischer, K. (1997) 'Between nature and nurture: The role of human agency in the epigenesis of intelligence', in R. Sternberg and E. Grigorenko (eds) *Intelligence, Heredity and Environment*. Cambridge: Cambridge University Press.

Biehl, J. (ed.) (1997) *The Murray Bookchin Reader*. London: Cassell.

Blackmore, S. (1999) *The Meme Machine*. Oxford: Oxford University Press.

Bland, L. and Doan, L. (1998) *Sexology Uncensored: The Documents of Sexual Science*. Oxford: Polity Press.

Boehm, C. (1997) 'Egalitarianism and political intelligence', in A. Whiten and R. Byrne (eds) *Machiavellian Intelligence II: Evaluations and Extensions*. Cambridge: Cambridge University Press.

Bookchin, M. (1982) *The Ecology of Freedom*. Palo Alto, CA: Cheshire Books.

Bookchin, M. (1989) *Remaking Society*. Montreal: Black Rose.

Bond, G. and Gilliam, A. (1994) *Social Construction of the Past: Representation as Power*. London: Routledge.

Bosma, H., Marmot, M., Hemingway, H. *et al*. (1997) 'Low job control and risk of coronary heart disease in Whitehall II (prospective cohort) study', *British Medical Journal*, 314, 22 February: 558–65.

Bowler, P. (1983) *Evolution: The History of an Idea*. Berkeley: University of California.

Bowler, P. (1988) *The Non-Darwinian Revolution: Reinterpreting a Historical Myth*. Baltimore, MD: Johns Hopkins University Press.

Bowler, P. (1990) *Charles Darwin: The Man and His Influence*. Cambridge: Cambridge University Press.

Boyd, R. and Richerson, J. (1985) *Culture and the Evolutionary Process*. Chicago: University of Chicago Press.

Braverman, H. (1974) *Labor and Monopoly Capital: The Degradation of Work in the Twentieth Century*. New York: Monthly Press.

Breen, R. and Goldthorpe, J. (1998) 'Class inequality and meritocracy: A critique of Saunders and an alternative analysis', *British Journal of Sociology*, 50(1), 1–27.

Brunner, E. (1996) 'The social and biological basis of cardiovascular disease in office workers', in E. Brunner, D. Blane and R. Wilkinson (eds) *Health and Social Organisation*. London: Routledge.

Brunner, E. (1997) 'Stress and the biology of inequality', *British Medical Journal*, 314, 1472–6.

Brunner, E., Davey-Smith, G., Marmot, M. *et al.* (1996) 'Childhood social circumstances and psychosocial and behavioural factors as determinants of plasma fibrinogen', *The Lancet*, 347, 13 April: 1008–13.

Buck-Morss, S. (1982) 'Socio-economic bias in Piaget's theory and its implications for cross-cultural studies', in S. Modgil and C. Modgil (eds) *Jean Piaget: Consensus and Controversy*. London: Holt, Rinehart and Winston. (Reprint of article in *Human Development*, 18, 1975.)

Burkhardt, F. (ed.) (1996) *Charles Darwin's Letters: A Selection 1825–1859*. Cambridge: Cambridge University Press.

Butterworth, G., Siegal, M., Newcombe, P. and Dorfmann, M. (1998) 'Young children's knowledge of the shape of the earth in Australia and England'. Paper presented to the Research in Child Development Conference, Washington, DC, 1997.

Byrne, R. (1995) *The Thinking Ape: Evolutionary Origins of Intelligence*. Oxford: Oxford University Press.

Byrne, R. and Whiten, A. (1988) *Machiavellian Intelligence: Social Expertise and the Evolution of Intellect in Monkeys, Apes and Humans*. Oxford: Oxford University Press.

Capra, F. (1983) *The Turning Point*. London: Fontana.

Carraher, T., Carraher, D. and Schliemann, A. (1985) 'Mathematics in the streets and in the schools', *British Journal of Developmental Psychology*, 3: 21–9.

Catton, W. (1998) 'Darwin, Durkheim and mutualism', *Advances in Human Ecology,* 7: 89–113.

Cavalli-Sforza, L. and Feldman, M. (1981) *Cultural Transmission and Evolution: A Quantitative Appraoch*. Princeton, NJ: Princeton University Press.

Chagnon, N. (1992) *The Last Days of Eden*. New York: Harcourt Brace Jovanovich.

Chitty, A. (1994) 'Marx, moral conscience and history', in C. Bertram and A. Chitty (eds) *Has History Ended?* Aldershot: Avebury.

Chorney, M., Chorney, K., Seese, N. *et al.* (1998) 'A quantitative trail locus associated with cognition ability in children', *Psychological Science*, 9(3): 159–66.

Cohen, G. (1978) *Karl Marx's Theory of History: A Defence*. Oxford: Clarendon Press.

Colborn, T., Myers, T. and Dumanoski, D. (1996) *Our Stolen Future*. Boston: Little, Brown.

Collier, A. (1994) *Critical Realism: An Introduction to Roy Bhaskar's Philosophy*. London: Verso.

Curry, O., Cronin, C. and Ashworth, J. (1996) 'Matters of life and death; the world view from evolutionary psychology', *Demos Quarterly*, 10.

Daniels, M., Devlin, B. and Roeder, K. (1997) 'Of genes and IQ', in B.

Devlin, S. Fienberg, D. Resnick and K. Roeder (eds) *Intelligence, Genes and Success: Scientists Respond to The Bell Curve.* New York: Copernicus.

Darwin, C. (1901) *The Descent of Man and Selection in Relation to Sex* (2nd edn). London: Murray. (First published in 1871.)

Darwin, C. (1968) *The Origin of Species by Natural Selection.* Harmondsworth: Penguin. (First published in 1859.)

Darwin, C. (1987a) 'Notebook M', in P. Barrett, P. Gautrey, S. Herbert, D. Kohn and S. Smith (eds) *Charles Darwin's Notebooks, 1836–1844.* New York: Cornell University Press. (First written in 1838.)

Darwin, C. (1987b) 'Notebook N', in P. Barrett, P. Gautrey, S. Herbert, D. Kohn and S. Smith (eds) *Charles Darwin's Notebooks, 1836–1844.* Cambridge: Cambridge University Press. (First written in 1838 and 1839.)

Darwin, C. (1987c) 'Old and useless notes', in P. Barrett, P. Gautrey, S. Herbert, D. Kohn and S. Smith (eds) *Charles Darwin's Notebooks, 1836–1844.* Cambridge: Cambridge University Press. (First written between 1838 and 1840.)

Darwin, C. (1998) *The Expression of the Emotions in Man and Animals.* London: HarperCollins. (First published in 1872.)

Dawkins, R. (1989) *The Selfish Gene.* Oxford: Oxford University Press.

Dennett, D. (1990) 'Memes and the exploitation of imagination', *Journal of Aesthetics and Art Criticism,* 48(2): 127–35.

Desmond, A. (1989) *The Politics of Evolution: Morphology, Medicine and Reform in Radical London.* Chicago: Chicago University Press.

Devlin, B., Daniels, M. and Roeder, K. (1997) 'The heritability of IQ', *Nature,* 388(6641): 31 July.

Dickens, P. (1992) *Society and Nature: Towards a Green Social Theory.* Hemel Hempstead: Harvester.

Dickens, P. (1996) *Reconstructing Nature: Alienation, Emancipation and the Division of Labour.* London: Routledge.

Donaldson, M. (1978) *Children's Minds.* London: Fontana.

Drouin, J.-M. and Bensaude-Vincent, B. (1996) 'Nature for the people', in N. Jardine, J. Secord and E. Spary (eds) *Cultures of Natural History.* Cambridge: Cambridge University Press.

Dyhouse, C. (1976) 'Social Darwinist ideas and the development of women's education in England 1880–1920', *History of Education,* 5(1): 41–58.

Eder, K. (1984) 'Learning and the evolution of social systems: An epigenetic perspective', in M. Schmid and F. Wuketits (eds) *Evolutionary Theory in Social Science.* Dordrecht: D. Reidel.

Eder, K. (1987) 'On the cultural origins and the historical formation of the traditional state: Some theoretical considerations', in W. Wostal (ed.)

On Social Evolution: Contributions to Anthropological Concepts. Horn, Austria: Berger.

Eder, K. (1999) 'Societies learn and yet the world is hard to change', *European Journal of Social Theory*, 2(2): 195–215.

Elias, N. (1994) *The Civilizing Process.* Oxford: Blackwell. (First published in 1939.)

Elson, D. (1979) 'Which way "out of the ghetto"?', *Capital and Class*, 9, Autumn: 97–117.

Engels, F. (1989) 'Duhring's revolution in science' in L. Feuer (ed.) *Marx and Engels: Basic Writings on Politics and Philosophy.* New York: Doubleday. (First published in 1878).

Erdal, D. and Whiten, A. (1996) 'Egalitarianism and Machiavellian intelligence in human evolution', in P. Mellars and K. Gibson (eds) *Modelling the Early Human Mind.* McDonald Institute Monographs. Cambridge: McDonald Institute for Archaeological Research.

Fischbach, G. (1992) 'Mind and brain', *Scientific American*, 267(3): 24–32.

Frank, A. (1972) 'The development of underdevelopment', in J. Cockroft, A. Frank and D. Johnson (eds) *Dependence and Underdevelopment: Latin America's Political Economy.* New York: Doubleday.

Freud, S. (1987) 'Civilisation and its discontents', in S. Dickson (ed.), *Civilisation, Society and Religion.* Pelican Freud Library Vol. 12. Harmondsworth: Penguin. (First published in 1930).

Frith, U. and Happé, F. (1999) 'Theory of mind and self-consciousness. What is it like to be autistic?', *Mind and Language*, 14(1): 1–22.

Fukuyama, F. (1992) *The End of History and the Last Man.* Harmondsworth: Penguin.

Fukuyama, F. (1999a) *The Great Disruption: Human Nature and the Reconstitution of Social Order.* London: Profile.

Fukuyama, F. (1999b) 'The end of history? Well, certainly the end of humans', *The Independent*, 16 June.

Gellner, E. (1988) *Plough, Sword and Book: The Structure of Human History.* London: Collins Harvill.

Giddens, A. (1984) *The Constitution of Society: Outline of the Theory of Structuration.* Oxford: Polity Press.

Goddard, A. (1998) 'Sense of self sets human beings apart', *Times Higher Education Supplement*, 11 September.

Goodwin, B. (1994) *How the Leopard Changed Its Spots.* London: Weidenfeld and Nicolson.

Gottlieb, G. (1992) *Individual Development and Evolution: The Genesis of Novel Behaviour.* Oxford: Oxford University Press.

Gould, S. (1977) 'Eternal metaphors of palaeontology', in A. Hallam (ed.) *Patterns of Evolution as Illustrated by the Fossil Record.* New York: Elsevier.

Gould, S. (1980) *Ever since Darwin*. Harmondsworth: Pelican.

Greenough, W., Black, J. and Wallace, C. (1993) 'Brain adaptation to experience', in M.H. Johnson (ed.) *Brain Development and Cognition*. Oxford: Blackwell.

Gruber, H. (1974) *Darwin on Man: A Psychological Study of Scientific Creativity*. New York: Dutton.

Habermas, J. (1996) 'The normative content of modernity', in W. Outhwaite (ed.) *The Habermas Reader*. Oxford: Polity Press.

Hacker, A. (1995) 'Caste, crime and precocity', in S. Fraser (ed.) *The Bell Curve Wars: Race, Intelligence and the Future of America*. London: Basic Books.

Hales, M. (1980) *Living Thinkwork: Where do Labour Processes Come From?* London: CSE Books.

Haraway, D. (1992) *Primate Visions: Gender, Race, and Nature in the World of Modern Science*. London: Verso.

Hayward, T. (1998) *Political Theory and Ecological Values*. Oxford: Polity Press.

Hawkins, M. (1997) *Social Darwinism in European and American Thought: Nature as Model and Nature as Threat*. Cambridge: Cambridge University Press.

Hegel, G. (1975) *Lectures on the Philosophy of World History*. Cambridge: Cambridge University Press.

Herrnstein, R. and Murray, C. (1994) *The Bell Curve: Intelligence and Class Structure in American Life*. New York: Free Press.

Heylighen, F. (1996) 'Evolution of memes on the network: From chain letters to the global brain', available from the author, Center 'Leo Apostel', Free University of Brussels, Pleinlaan 2, B–1050, Brussels, Belgium.

Hirst, P. (1976) *Social Evolution and Sociological Categories*. London: Allen & Unwin.

Hirst, P. (1994) 'The evolution of consciousness: Identity and personality in historical perspective', *Economy and Society*, 23(1): 47–65.

Ho, M.-W. (1998) *Genetic Engineering: Dream or Nightmare?* Bath: Gateway Books.

Hodgson, G. (1993) *Economics and Evolution: Bringing Life Back into Economics*. Oxford: Polity Press.

Hofstadter, R. (1959) *Social Darwinism in American Thought*. New York: Braziller.

Humphrey, N. (1976) 'The social function of intellect', in P. Bateson and R. Hinde (eds) *Growing Points in Ethology*. Cambridge: Cambridge University Press.

Hunt, E. (1997) 'The concept and utility of intelligence', in B. Devlin, S. Fienberg, D. Resnick and K. Roeder (eds) *Intelligence, Genes and Success*. New York: Copernicus.

Ingold, T. (1986) *The Appropriation of Nature: Essays on Human Ecology and Social Relations*. Manchester: Manchester University Press.

Jablonska, E. and Lamb, M. (1995) *Epigenetic Inheritance and Evolution*. Oxford: Oxford University Press.

James, O. (1997) *Britain on the Couch*. London: Century.

Jones, G. (1980) *Social Darwinism and English Thought: The Interaction Between Biological and Social Theory*. Brighton: Harvester.

Judis, J. (1995) 'Hearts of darkness', in S. Fraser (ed.) *The Bell Curve Wars: Race, Intelligence and the Future of America*. London: Basic Books.

Junge, K. (1993) 'Evolutionary processes in the economy', in W. Outhwaite and T. Bottomore (eds) *The Blackwell Dictionary of 20th Century Social Thought*. Oxford: Blackwell.

Keating, D. and Hertzman, C. (eds) (1999) *Developmental Health and the Wealth of Nations: Social, Biological and Educational Dynamics*. New York: Guilford Press.

Kerr, C., Dunlop, J., Harbison, F. and Myers, C. (1960) *Industrialism and Industrial Man*. London: Heinemann.

Knauft, B. (1991) 'Violence and sociality in human evolution', *Current Anthropology*, 32: 391–428.

Kohn, M. and Schooler, C. (1973) 'Occupational experience and psychological functioning: an assessment of reciprocal effects', *American Sociological Review*, 38: 97–118.

Kropotkin, P. (1987) *Mutual Aid: A Factor of Evolution*. London: Freedom Press. (First published in 1902.)

Lambert, H. and Rose, H. (1996) 'Disembodied knowledge? Making sense of medical science', in A. Irwin and B. Wynne (eds) *Misunderstanding Science? The Public Reconstruction of Science and Technology*. Cambridge: Cambridge University Press.

Lerner, D. (1958) *The Passing of Traditional Society*. New York: Free Press.

Lewontin, R. (1982) 'Organism and environment', in H. Plotkin (ed.) *Learning, Development and Culture*. Chichester: Wiley.

Lewontin, R. (1991) *The Doctrine of DNA: Biology as Ideology*. Harmondsworth: Penguin.

Lind, M. (1995) 'Brave New Right', in S. Fraser (ed.) *The Bell Curve Wars: Race, Intelligence and the Future of America*. London: Basic Books.

Lovallo, W. (1997) *Stress and Health: Biological and Psychological Interactions*. London: Sage.

Lubbock, J. (1875) *The Origin of Civilisation and the Primitive Condition of Man* (3rd edn). London: Longmans, Green.

Luhmann, N. (1982) *The Differentiation of Society*. New York: Columbia University Press.

Luhmann, N. (1989) *Ecological Communication*. Oxford: Polity Press.

Lumsden, C. and Wilson, E. (1981) *Genes, Mind and Culture: The Co-evolutionary Process*. Cambridge, MA: Harvard University Press.

Lynch, A. (1996) *Thought Contagion: How Belief Spreads Through Society*. New York: Basic Books.

MacLean, P. (1983) 'A triangular brief on the evolution of brain and law' in M. Gruter and P. Bohannan (eds) *Law, Biology and Culture*. Santa Barbara, CA: Ross-Erikson.

MacLean, P. (1990) *The Triune Brain in Evolution*. New York: Plenum.

Macnicol, J. (1987) 'In pursuit of the underclass', *Journal of Social Policy*, 16: 293–318.

Malik, K. (1996) *The Meaning of Race: Race, History and Culture in Western Society*. London: Macmillan.

Mallet, S. (1975) *The New Working Class*. Nottingham: Spokesman.

Mann, M. (1973) *Workers on the Move: The Sociology of Relocation*. Cambridge: Cambridge University Press.

Markovic, M. (1991) 'Human nature', in T. Bottomore (ed.) *A Dictionary of Marxist Thought*. Oxford: Blackwell.

Marmot, M. and Wadsworth, M. (eds) (1997) 'Fetal and early childhood environment: long-term health implications', *British Medical Bulletin*, 53(1), January.

Marshall, G. and Swift, A. (1996) 'Merit and mobity: A reply to Peter Saunders', *Sociology*, 30(2): 375–86.

Martin, P. (1997) *The Sickening Mind*. London: Harper Collins.

Martinez Allier, J. (1987) *Ecological Economics: Energy, Environment and Society*. Oxford: Blackwell.

Marx, K. (1973) *Grundrisse*. Harmondsworth: Penguin.

Marx, K. (1975a) 'Economic and philosophical manuscripts', in L. Colletti (ed.) *Karl Marx: Early Writings*. Harmondsworth: Penguin. (First published in 1844.).

Marx, K. (1975b) 'Concerning Feuerbach', in L.Colletti (ed.) *Karl Marx: Early Writings*. Harmondsworth: Penguin. (First published in 1845.)

Marx, K. (1976) *Capital: Volume 1*. Harmondsworth: Penguin.

Marx, K. and Engels, F. (1970) *The German Ideology* (ed. C. Arthur). London: Lawrence and Wishart. (First published in 1932.)

Maryanski, A. (1992) 'The last ancestor: An ecological network model on the origins of human sociality', *Advances in Human Ecology*, 1: 1–32.

Maryanski, A. and Turner, J. (1992) *The Social Cage: Human Nature and the Evolution of Society*. Stanford, CA: Stanford University Press.

Matthews, F. (1991) *The Ecological Self*. London: Routledge.

Maynard Smith, J. (1998) *Shaping Life: Genes, Embryos and Evolution*. London: Weidenfeld and Nicolson.

McGue, M. (1997) 'The democracy of the genes', *Nature*, 38, 31 July: 417–18.

McLellan, D. (ed.) (1977) *Karl Marx: Selected Writings*. Oxford: Oxford University Press.

Mead, G.H. (1934) *Mind, Self and Society*. Chicago: University of Chicago Press.

Mennell, S. (1989) *Norbert Elias: Civilization and Human Self-Image.* Oxford: Blackwell.

Mies, M. and Shiva, V. (1993) *Ecofeminism.* London: Zed Books.

Miller, J. (1997) 'A cultural-psychology perspective on intelligence', in R. Sternberg and E. Grigorenko (eds) *Intelligence, Heredity and Environment.* Cambridge: Cambridge University Press.

Montagu, A. (1997) *Man's Most Dangerous Myth: The Fallacy of Race.* Walnut Creek, CA: AltaMira Press. (First published in 1942.)

Montgomery, S., Bartley, M., Cook, D. and Wadsworth, M. (1996) 'Health and social precursors of unemployment in young men in Great Britain', *Journal of Epidemiology and Community Health*, 50: 415–22.

Montgomery, S., Bartley, M. and Wilkinson, R. (1997) 'Family conflict and slow growth', *Archives of the Diseases of Childhood*, 77: 326–30.

Naess, A. (1989) *Ecology, Community and Lifestyle.* Cambridge: Cambridge University Press.

Neisser, U., Boodoo, G., Bouchard, T. *et al.* (1996) 'Intelligence: Knowns and unknowns', *American Psychologist*, 55(2): 77–101.

Nelson, R. and Winter, S. (1982) *An Evolutionary Theory of Economic Change.* Cambridge, MA: Harvard University Press.

Nesse, R. and Williams, G. (1995) *Evolution and Healing: The New Science of Darwinian Medicine.* London: Phoenix.

Nesse, R. and Williams, R. (1996) 'Is there an evolutionist in the house?', *Demos Quarterly*, 10: 25–7.

Nisbett, R. (1995) 'Race, IQ and scientism', in S. Fraser (ed.) *The Bell Curve Wars: Race, Intelligence and the Future of America.* London: Basic Books.

O'Connor, M. (1994) *Is Capitalism Sustainable? Political Economy and the Politics of Ecology.* New York: Guilford Press.

O'Connor, M. (1996) 'The second contradiction of capitalism', in T. Benton (ed.) *The Greening of Marxism.* New York: Guilford Press.

Offer, J. (1999) 'Spencer's future of welfare: A vision eclipsed', *Sociological Review*, 47(1): 136–62.

Outram, D. (1996) 'New spaces in natural history', in N. Jardine, J. Secord and E. Spary (eds) *Cultures of Natural History.* Cambridge: Cambridge University Press.

Overy, C. (1997) *Charles Darwin: His Life, Journeys and Discoveries.* London: English Heritage.

Parsons, T. (1966) *Societies: Evolutionary and Comparative Perspectives.* New York: Prentice Hall.

Patel, C. (1996) *The Complete Guide to Stress Management.* London: Vermilion.

Patterson, O. (1995) 'For whom the bell curves', in S. Fraser (ed.) *The Bell Curve Wars: Race, Intelligence and the Future of America.* London: Basic Books.

Peel, J. (1972) 'Introduction', in J. Peel (ed.) *Herbert Spencer on Social Evolution: Selected Writings*. Chicago: University of Chicago Press.

Perrin, R. (1976) 'Herbert Spencer's four theories of social evolution', *American Journal of Sociology*, 81: 1339–59.

Piaget, J. (1971) *Biology and Knowledge: An Essay on the Relations between Organic Regulations and Cognitive Processes*. Edinburgh: Edinburgh University Press.

Pinker, S. (1997) *How the Mind Works*. Harmondsworth: Allen Lane/Penguin Press.

Plomin, R., McClearn, G., Smith, D. *et al.* (1994) 'DNA markers associated with high versus low IQs: The Quantitative Tract Loci (QTL) Project', *Behaviour Genetics*, 24(2): 107–18.

Poster, M. (1979) *Sartre's Marxism*. London: Pluto.

Power, C. and Hertzman, C. (1999) 'Health, well-being, and coping skills', in D. Keating and C. Hertzman (eds) *Developmental Health and the Wealth of Nations: Social, Biological and Educational Dynamics*. New York: Guilford Press.

Ramos, D. (1995) 'Paradise miscalculated', in S. Fraser (ed.) *The Bell Curve Wars: Race, Intelligence and the Future of America*. London: Basic Books.

Ramsey, H. and Haworth, N. (1984) *Prefigurative Socialism and the Strategies of Transition*. Discussion Paper 12. Glasgow: Centre for Research in Industrial Democracy and Participation, University of Glasgow.

Reeves, J. (1999) 'Models sell their eggs for "perfect" baby', *Observer*, 24 October.

Richardson, K. (1998) *The Origins of Human Potential: Evolution, Development and Psychology*. London: Routledge.

Ridley, M. (1994) *The Red Queen: Sex and the Evolution of Human Nature*. Harmondsworth: Penguin.

Robertson, I. (1999) *Mind Sculpture: Your Brain's Untapped Potential*. London: Bantam.

Rohe, J. (1997) *A Bicentennial Malthusian Essay: Conservation, Population and the Indifference to Limits*. Traverse City: Rhodes and Easton.

Rose, S. (1997) *Lifelines: Biology, Freedom, Determinism*. Harmondsworth: Penguin.

Rose, S., Lewontin, R. and Kamin, L. (1984) *Not in Our Genes: Biology, Ideology and Human Nature*. Harmondsworth: Pelican.

Rosen, J. and Lane, C. (1995) 'The sources of the bell curve', in S. Fraser (ed.) *The Bell Curve Wars: Race, Intelligence and the Future of America*. London: Basic Books.

Rostow, W. (1960) *The Stages of Economic Growth: A Non-Communist Manifesto*. Cambridge: Cambridge University Press.

Rowbotham, S., Segal, L. and Wainwright, H. (1979) *Beyond the Fragments: Feminism and the Making of Socialism*. London: Merlin.

Rudy, A. (1998) 'Ecology and anthropology in the work of Murray Bookchin: Problems of theory and evidence', *Capitalism, Nature, Socialism*, 9(2): 57–90.

Runciman, W. (1998) 'The selectionist paradigm and its implications for sociology', *Sociology*, 32(1): 163–88.

Ruse, M. (1996) *Monad to Man: The Concept of Progress in Evolutionary Biology*. Cambridge, MA: Harvard University Press.

Sanderson, S. (1990) *Social Evolutionism: A Critical History*. Oxford: Blackwell.

Sanderson, S. (1994) 'Evolutionary materialism: A theoretical strategy for the study of social evolution', *Sociological Perspectives*, 37(1): 42–73.

Saunders, P. (1995) *Capitalism: A Social Audit*. Buckingham: Open University Press.

Saunders, P. (1996) *Unequal But Fair? A Study of Class Barriers in Britain*. Choice in Welfare Series No. 28. London: Institute of Economic Affairs.

Saunders, P. (1997) 'Social mobility in Britain: An empirical examination of two competing explanations', *Sociology*, 31: 161–88.

Savage, M. and Egerton, M. (1997) 'Social mobility, individual ability and class inequality', *Sociology*, 31(4): 645–72.

Schmidt, A. (1971) *The Concept of Nature in Marx*. London: New Left Books.

Secord, A. (1996) 'Artisan botany', in N. Jardine, J. Secord and E. Spary (eds) *Cultures of Natural History*. Cambridge: Cambridge University Press.

Seligman, M. (1975) *Helplessness*. San Francisco: Freeman.

Selye, H. (1984) *The Stress of Life*. New York: McGraw Hill.

Shatz, C. (1992) 'The developing brain', *Scientific American*, 267: 35–41.

Shteir, A. (1996) *Cultivating Women, Cultivating Science: Flora's Daughters and Botany in England 1760–1860*. Baltimore, MD: Johns Hopkins University Press.

Smelser, N. (1959) *Social Change in the Industrial Revolution: An Application of Theory to the Lancashire Cotton Industry 1770–1840*. London: Routledge & Kegan Paul.

Sober, E. (1999) 'Altruism, biology and society: An interview with Elliott Sober', *Imprints*, 3(3): 197–213.

Sohn-Rethel, A. (1975) 'Science as alienated consciousness', *Radical Science*, 2/3: 65–101.

Sowell, T. (1995) 'Ethnicity and IQ', in S. Fraser (ed.) *The Bell Curve Wars: Race, Intelligence and the Future of America*. London: Basic Books.

Spearman, C. (1927) *The Abilities of Man: Their Nature and Measurement*. London: Macmillan.

Spencer, H. (1857) *Principles of Biology*, Vol. 2. London: Williams and Norgate.

Spencer, H. (1893) *The Principles of Sociology*, Vol. 1. London: Williams and Norgate.

Spencer, H. (1898) *Principles of Biology*, 2 vols. New York: Appleton.

Spencer, H. (1904) *An Autobiography*, Vol. 1. London: Williams and Norgate.

Spencer, H. (1996) *Essays: Scientific, Political and Speculative. Vol. 1.* London: Routledge. (First published in 1857.)

Stedman Jones, G. (1971) *Outcast London: A Study in the Relationship between Classes in Victorian Society*. Oxford: Clarendon Press.

Steele, E., Lindley, R. and Blanden, R. (1998) *Lamarck's Signature: How Retrogenes are Changing Darwin's Natural Selection Paradigm*. St. Leonards, NSW: Allen & Unwin.

Stepan, N. (1982) *The Idea of Race in Science: Great Britain 1800–1960*. London: Macmillan.

Sternberg, R. (1985) 'Introduction: What is an information-processing approach to human abilities?', in R. Sternberg (ed.) *Human Abilities: An Information-Processing Approach*. New York: Freeman.

Steward, J. (1955) *Theory of Culture Change: The Methodology of Multi-linear Evolution*. Urbana: University of Illinois Press.

Sylva, K. (1997) 'Critical periods in childhood learning', *British Medical Bulletin*, 53(1): 185–97.

Tobach, E., Gianutsos, J., Topoff, H. and Groff, C. (1974) *The Four Horsemen: Racism, Sexism, Militarism and Social Darwinism*. New York: Behavioral Publications.

Toennies, F. (1955) *Community and Association*. London: Routledge & Kegan Paul.

Touraine, A., Durand, C., Pecant, D. and Willener, A. (1965) *Workers' Attitudes to Technical Change*. Paris: Organization for Economic Cooperation and Development.

Townsend, P. and Davidson, N. (1980) *The Health Divide – The Black Report*. Harmondsworth: Penguin.

Trigger, B. (1998) *Sociocultural Evolution: Calculation and Contingency*. Oxford: Blackwell.

Turner, J. (1985) *Herbert Spencer: A Renewed Appreciation*. Beverley Hills, CA: Sage.

Waddington, C. (1957) *The Strategy of the Genes*. London: Allen & Unwin.

Waddington, C. (1975) *The Evolution of an Evolutionist*. Edinburgh: Edinburgh University Press.

Wallace, A.R. (1869) *The Malay Archipelago*, 2 vols. London: Macmillan.

Whitehead, M. (1987) *The Health Divide – Inequalities in Health*. London: Health Education Council.

Whiten, A. (1999) 'The evolution of deep social mind in humans', in M. Corballis and S. Lea (eds) *The Descent of Mind*. Oxford: Oxford University Press.

Whiten, A. and Byrne, R (eds) (1997) *Machiavellian Intelligence II: Extensions and Evaluations*. Cambridge: Cambridge University Press.

Wilkinson, R. (1996) *Unhealthy Societies: The Afflictions of Inequality*. London: Routledge.

Wilkinson, R. (1997) 'What health tells us about society', *Soundings*, special issue, *The Next Ten Years*: 125–42.

Williams, R. (1976a) 'Evolution', in *Keywords: A Vocabulary of Culture and Society*. London: Fontana.

Williams, R. (1976b) 'Progressive', in *Keywords: A Vocabulary of Culture and Society*. London: Fontana.

Wills, C. (1989) *The Wisdom of the Genes: New Pathways in Evolution*. New York: Basic Books.

Wills, C. (1993) *The Runaway Brain: The Evolution of Human Uniqueness*. London: Flamingo.

Wolfe, A. (1995) 'Has there been a cognitive revolution in America?', in S. Fraser (ed.) *The Bell Curve Wars: Race, Intelligence and the Future of America*. London: Basic Books.

Woods, A. and Grant, T. (1995) *Reason in Revolt*. London: Welred.

World Bank (1993) *World Development Report 1993: Investing in Health*. Oxford: Oxford University Press.

Wrangham, R. and Peterson, D. (1997) *Demonic Males: Apes and the Origins of Human Violence*. London: Bloomsbury.

Wright, R. (1994) *The Moral Animal: Why We Are the Way We Are*. London: Abacus.

Wright, R. (1996) 'The dissent of woman. What feminists can learn from Darwinism', *Demos Quarterly*, 10: 18–24.

Wynne-Edwards, V. (1986) *Evolution through Group Selection*. Oxford: Blackwell.

Index